WORDS TO LOVE BY

KAREN L. BONCELA

WORDS TO LOVE BY by Karen L. Boncela

ISBN 13:   978-0615572239
ISBN 10:   0615572235
LCCN: 2011962886

Book and Cover designed by Ellie Searl

PRINTED IN THE USA

PURPLE KNIGHT PRESS
NAPERVILLE, IL

THIS BOOK IS DEDICATED to my children, JR, Gina, and Valerie, who inspired me to make some of the most important choices in my life; to my sister, Nancy, whose generosity allowed me my freedom; to Eddie's nephew, Tommy…without his suggestion to Eddie, our paths may have never crossed; and of course to my Eddie, who lets me be exactly me and loves me anyway…………..no matter what.

CONTENTS

KAREN L. BONCELA

O N E

I T'S THE MIDDLE OF July and I'm looking out my patio door into my big beautiful backyard. I can see the garden that we built; it makes me smile every time I look and see just how wonderfully our garden is thriving; it's the best that I've ever had and I'm not surprised! My garden seems to be a reflection of my life.

This has been the best year of my life. I have learned so much about myself and other people; I think that I'm the smartest that I have ever been. The most important thing that I have learned is that you never know what someone else is living unless you are in their shoes living it. I will never judge anyone again and will never assume to know what they might be dealing with in their life.

July is a special month for us. We first met last year in July; in fact, it was July 18th, my birthday.

If I can make you feel even a tiny bit of the emotion that I have felt this past year, it will warm your heart and make you believe that anything is possible and that love can happen at the most unexpected time in your life and that you are never too old, or too tired, or too disillusioned to find true love.

I'll go back now and tell you a little bit about how I got to this point in my life.

I'm a middle-aged woman, wow that sounds old. But anyway, let's just say that when I celebrate birthdays each year, my children have taken a habit now of asking me how old I am because it's been so long since I've admitted to or for that matter, behaved like many people my age do. It's all in good fun, of course, and I'm a huge believer of that old phrase that you are as young as you feel............and I feel young!

I have three wonderful and different grown children that I adore, and I have one beautiful and smart and unique grandson. Last July, I was married for thirty-one years to a man named David whom I met when I was a youngster in high school. We thought that we were so smart back then; it makes me laugh now. He was fiercely possessive of me and I think now that I confused that with love. I thought that he would always take good care of me. I lived at home with my parents until I married. I had a bit of a rocky relationship with my mom and planning my wedding seemed the perfect way to get out on my own.

Our marriage started out pretty well; we went on a very romantic honeymoon to Acapulco, Mexico. I remember him telling me once in Mexico, how beautiful my body was to him. I don't think that he ever told me that again, sad really. Once we got into the routine of our lives, our time was spent working, saving for a home and socializing with friends. I used to wonder how he could drink the quantity of alcohol that he did and still get us home in one piece. He would actually pass out sometimes in front of our home once we got there.

We went on to have our three children in a matter of four years. I was a very busy mom for many years. I felt like a single mom as far as the parenting responsibilities went. David worked all the time. He owned his own business for a while and seemed to be a very hard worker. Once I had my children, I realized that I could not continue to socialize in the same way that we used to, where lots of drinking was involved. I could not care for my children the way I wanted to if I had a hangover. So I stopped and I concentrated on keeping a nice home and caring for my children. I stayed at home with them while David worked and went out and socialized......at the bar, without me.

I could see as the years progressed that his drinking was becoming a problem for him, in every aspect of his life. His work suffered and so did I. And so did the kids. David was never around for them. Kids really need their dad. I can remember my son begging me to get his dad to talk to him about important things as he grew up but David just didn't have time. He never heard what I was saying or just didn't care enough to make any changes. I realize now that he had always been a selfish person and could never really see anything beyond himself.

We argued a lot; he said a lot of mean things to me, at first just under his breath so that the kids didn't hear him. Really mean words that were meant just for me. He would call me a bitch and a nag and a pain in his ass. Eventually, he didn't even try to shelter the kids from the mean things that he would say to me, he just let loose with fits of rage and verbal abuse, always directed at me. In his mind, I was the reason for everything and anything that was wrong in his life. Of course this behavior upset the children. I was there to try to calm them and unfortunately, back then, I used to think that it was my responsibility to make excuses for his tirades.

I would tell them, "Your dad had a rough day at work today." or "He doesn't really mean what he's saying, he's just upset."

He would come home drunk late at night, crawl into bed next to me and mumble how he wanted to shoot me dead and be rid of me. The frightening thing was that he owned several guns. I had tried many times to have him get rid of them but he wouldn't hear of it. I would pretend that I was sleeping so as not to provoke him any more than he already was. I would hold my breath until I knew that he was asleep. I was afraid that if he knew that I was awake, he would start a scene and upset the whole household. I did whatever I could to keep a bit of sanity in all our lives. I really just wanted the house to remain quiet for the kids' sake. They were always my first concern.

I can remember one time when he came home late; I was sleeping and he just came into our room and threw our whole mattress onto the floor with me in it for no particular reason.

One of the worst parts of living with an alcoholic is their bad memory. They can wake up the day after being a monster to you and not remember a thing. The morning after, David had no recall of what he had done the night before and I didn't want to bring it up for fear that he would rage once again. As the recipient of this awful behavior, trust me, you don't forget. This dysfunction went on for several years before I realized that I could not subject my children or myself to this kind of behavior anymore so I started researching treatment plans for him in the hopes that he would choose to get help and stop the drinking. By this time, David had also started using cocaine, which made his behavior even more unpredictable and frightening.

I had a brother-in-law who was a recovering alcoholic who helped me to arrange an "intervention" of sorts to get David to go into treatment for his addictions. He agreed to get help, that he would do it for me. I realize now what a mistake that was. David needed to get help for HIMSELF, to benefit HIMSELF, not for me. He was in the hospital for thirty days. We checked him in right after Christmas one year.

To say that time was difficult is such an understatement. I had three small children to care for while I tried to keep David's business alive. I visited him every day at the hospital, which was forty minutes away from our home. It's amazing what we can endure in tough times. My daily schedule during those thirty days was like I had never experienced before or since. My son was five years old at the time, my daughters were two and just under one year old. I hired two housekeepers, a woman and her daughter who offered me some help caring for my children and for my home while I went to David's auto service and gas station all day long and tried to pretend that I knew what I was doing in trying to keep it afloat. I had to lie to all his work associates about where David was, just saying that he was in the hospital with some health issues.

I would come home in the evening, see the children for a bit, and then go to the hospital to see David who was abusive to me still, threatening to leave treatment. I was so affected myself by the alcoholism that I thought this was what I needed to do, come hell or high water! I was so preoccupied that I can remember one night on my way to the hospital just about running a person over with my car!

I felt so lost ……..and afraid……. and alone, I didn't know what else to do.

After thirty days, David came home. I thought that it would be the beginning of a new and alcohol and drug free life and all would be wonderful. Just the thought now of what lay ahead for all of us, makes me shudder now. Life's challenges can be so incredibly difficult.

I had a wonderful sponsor in Al Anon, who helped me get through the first year. I knew that I had to learn how to respond to David in a totally different way than I had before in order to get better myself, which in turn would help him too.

I hardly knew where to begin. I called my sponsor several times a day for advice on how to handle situations that came up every day while trying to recover. It took such incredible thought and effort on my part to choose to behave differently; to react differently to him, which by the way, pissed him off to the degree of rage. He'd always been able to manipulate me into whatever he wanted me to do and to think. I was beginning to change into a healthier minded person, started to gain my self-confidence. I'd started dating him at such a young age, that I'd never really been a confident and mature woman on my own, always leaning on him to complete me. I was only fourteen years old when I met him. David did not like it one bit that I was changing...........and getting healthier mentally, without him. I knew that I had to do it for my children's sake and for my own.

David and I attended some group therapy together, which was a follow up kind of thing that was an extension of his in-hospital treatment. My sponsor was one of the group leaders whom I confided in. Up until David's treatment, I had become quite afraid of him and his violent behavior and his reactions to me and unfortunately, that had not changed with his sobriety, so I began to use these therapy sessions as my safe place to vent and to verbalize to him what was on my mind. I figured that he wouldn't threaten me in front of other people. David would be asked questions at these sessions and would most often lie to everyone there, talking about what he was doing to change his behavior which had led up to the drinking and drugs. Sadly, in reality, David was not doing what he should have been to get himself well, in fact, nothing at all ... I often wondered then and still now how he managed to stay sober because he was and tragically, really still is, so profoundly sad and unhappy. He really may as well drink, he'd probably feel better, or at least, he wouldn't care about how unhappy he is.

There were several times in the car on the way home from our therapy that were filled with David's yelling at me.

"How dare you tell them about our personal lives?"

He actually stopped the car more than one time and said, "Get out of the fucking car right now before I throw you out!"

I cowered in the corner of the car and dared to stay, not saying anything as I hoped that his rage would pass. All that I had said was the truth.

It was because of David's lies that I lost my sponsor. I remember when she phoned me and told me that as she listened to David at meetings, knowing that he was lying to everyone there and to himself, she realized that she could not be a part of it, that I would have to find another sponsor.

And so the time passed............ and I kept hoping and praying that David would help himself with the information he'd been given in treatment, things he knew he could do for himself to get well. I was very busy, caring for my children and getting myself well, in my head. I even started a new Al Anon group at my church and ran meetings, trying to help other people in my same situation, which in turn, helped me to get healthy and stronger emotionally.

David lost his business shortly after his sobriety, despite my efforts to keep it alive while he'd been in treatment. His parents helped us to keep our home, which we almost lost too, all consequences of his addictions.

More years passed by and all the while I waited for David to feel better, to be kinder, to be happier, and to be healthier. I was always there for him, trying to encourage him and reminding him of all the blessings in our lives that we could be grateful for. We had three wonderful healthy children and David had found his way to working for someone else and brought home a substantial paycheck. He could never see the good though. He seemed to only see what his life lacked instead.

After we were married for twenty-five years, and at David's suggestion, we seemed to be doing well enough financially to consider buying a new home. We had lived in a very small, three bedroom, one bathroom house and had always considered it our first home. It was quite cramped for the five of us; all our children were still home with us. I thought that maybe this move would be good for us. I thought that it would be moral boosting to David to see what we could provide our family together, so we took the plunge. We watched step by step as our new home was built to our specifications. We would drive out to the site of the new home frequently and would be so excited as we saw it go up step by step. I felt hopeful for the first time in a long time.

But once we moved into our new home, it wasn't long before David's old behavior appeared.

He was totally absent for our children where it counted. He never really spoke to them about anything of significance. He was bothered really when they needed help with anything because he was constantly focused only on himself.

And still more years passed by. My children were young adults. David and I had become much more distant. He was just so unhappy all the time. Still to this day, I don't know how I stayed as long as I did.

A couple of years after we had moved into our new home, I just decided in my head that I was going to be happy in my life, no matter what. I didn't know if that would be with David or not, but I really never thought that I would have the courage to make a move towards divorce. The thought of my kids moving out and leaving me alone with their dad horrified me. I was so afraid that he would bring me down and make me as unhappy as he had become.

I decided to make a career change. In my previous job, I had worked mostly with women. In my new job, there was more of a mix of men and women. It was probably one of the best things that I could have done for myself. It began to feel liberating to have new friends that were just mine. I looked forward to going to work; it was such a nice break from the sadness and loneliness I felt at home. And yes, there was some flirting in the workplace which for me was eye-opening. There's no doubt that another man finding me attractive and treating me with kindness and respect felt good. It felt damn good!

I began to think that maybe I could muster up the courage to make a huge change in my life; that maybe I could be strong enough to be without David and all the grief associated with him.

T W O

I HAD BEGUN TO realize just how lonely a marriage can be. David did the majority of his socializing without me and by this point I looked forward to the times that he would go out and leave me alone. It was peaceful at least. I didn't have to listen to him complaining about the kids, the neighbors, his work associates, his job, his family, the house... the list went on and on.

There were so many times during our marriage that I had wondered just exactly what David was doing when he went out every Friday night to hang out with his friends.

When I first asked, "Who are you hanging out with and what exactly are you doing?"

He responded, "I'm just going out to eat and play pool with my buddies, I work hard all week and need to unwind!"

I could never figure out why he felt so obligated to do this more than once a week while his family was here at home, but I grew to accept it and not even question it anymore. I'm certain in after thought now, that he was probably handling himself in a way that would make many think that he was not married at all.

Early on, when he was drinking and using drugs, I many times thought about trying to follow him to see just exactly what he was up to. I'm grateful still today for the fact that I had three children at home that I would not leave alone. If it weren't for the kids, I probably would have followed him, which I realize now is so sick. Because whatever we are meant to know in this lifetime will come to us with no effort on our part.

As the years passed and David went out on his own, I got to the point where I absolutely didn't care where he was going or what he was doing; only that it gave me a break from the unhappiness he exuded.

But for so many years, I continued to believe that I could make things better between us, that I could make our relationship healthier. That's all part of the disease called addiction; often times it's the person who lives with the addicted person who is just as sick and messed up as the actual addicted person. I realize now that the only person I can change is myself and the only person I have control over is me.

I kept trying though. I thought ok, he's a man, aren't they all the same? I can make this work! Damnit! Won't it be just the same with any man?

I even tried everything when it came to our sex lives. I thought that if I could liven that up, perhaps everything else would follow. It became so incredibly disappointing though, from his lack of wanting to please me to his impotence. I realize now that our sex life was never very good, not even near that. In this area, like all others in his life, he was too selfish to think about anyone but himself. It had become a chore.............but I remember thinking "wow" It's been several months since we've had sex so I would initiate it just so I could tell myself that we did do it occasionally, and that our marriage was ok.

I finally realized after many, many disappointments in the bedroom on top of all the other abuse that it was over. I couldn't even undress in front of him anymore.

I didn't trust him and I'm not sure now if I ever did one hundred percent. I couldn't trust him with any part of me, inside or out.

I remember telling him after he had stopped drinking years earlier, that it would take a long time for me to trust him again and right away he thought I meant trusting him with other women, when that was not what I meant at all. I should have realized then that the reason he thought that way was because there were infidelity issues on his part. I still to this day don't understand how he could live with himself with all the lies and deception through the years. I don't know how he could sleep at night.

I meant that I couldn't trust him with any part of me, any part of who I was. I couldn't trust him with the thoughts inside my head. I couldn't even trust him enough to tell him what I would have liked in the bedroom. How can you possibly be intimate with someone you can't trust? Isn't that what intimacy is?

I can remember driving to work one day when I realized that it was over. After being married to David for thirty years, it finally hit me all of a sudden, like a slap in the face. There was no doubt that every part of my marriage was over........... it was shocking the way it hit me.

I had to pull off to the side of the road to try and compose myself. I just sat there and cried. I felt empty inside. It was devastating and incredibly sad. I began to realize how much time had passed where I had felt unhappy with him. I began to realize how much time I had wasted!

Still......I didn't know how I would have the courage to do what I realized now that I should do, and absolutely should have done many years before. Up until this point, I had never thought that divorce was even an option.

I recently watched an interview on TV of a young woman who was held captive for many years by a man who abused her in every way. Through the years that he kept her with him, she had several opportunities to run but never did.

The interviewer asked her, "Why didn't you get away, why didn't you run when you had a chance?"

She replied simply. "Leaving was not an option."

Most people would not understand that. I do because of my experience with David. I was married for life, I thought, divorce just not an option.

I thought that my only way out of this marriage would be if David were to die. I often thought about how that might happen. I thought about what a blessing it would be for me and my children if he were to just go away that way and leave us alone. We could all live a calm and peaceful life.

I never really thought about hurting him myself because he was on such a path of self-destruction, I thought he would likely bring harm to himself. I thought he might give himself a heart attack when he was having one of his fits of rage or that he might put himself into the hospital because of his lack of care of his own health. And because of his dishonest dealings, I even thought that he might end up in jail.

I began to say to myself, "How long am I going to hang around and watch him self-destruct?"

It's hard for someone who is living a normal life with reasonable and level headed people to imagine the kind of behavior that I tolerated. His tirades were insane. One summer day, David and I and the kids went to a major league baseball game. It started out with all of us laughing and enjoying each other's company. The game was canceled because of rain and we got lost on the way home which was more than enough for David to lose control. He ended up walking away from all of us, in the middle of a very bad neighborhood with car doors open, in the middle of the street! As he got out of the car, he was screaming obscenities. There were people looking at us, wondering what was wrong. The kids and I were horrified. There was a car full of us. My daughter's fiancé was with us and so was my grandson. I couldn't believe that David would humiliate himself like that in front of all of us. I felt so bad for my grandson especially, being a witness to his grandfather's insanity.

I realize now that we should have left him there in that bad neighborhood but I was so caught up in the insanity that we drove around looking for him and told him to get back in the car with us. He got back in the car, cursing at us still.

David was diabetic and most often ignored the fact. His diet was horrible. I envisioned him losing a limb or perhaps going blind because of the denial of his illness. I thought about just how stuck I would be with him as he grew older and sicker. How could I ever back away if he were very ill? What kind of person would I be? And then I would feel guilty for wishing him dead. But just how long could I hang around just waiting for the next bad thing to happen?

So I filled my days with busy things, working at my job, working around my house, going out with my friends occasionally, doing things with my children, and tolerating him and his insanity. I covered up for David all the time and I made excuses for his behavior.

My children were adults now and certainly didn't need me the way they used to and I was proud of them for that, all of them making their way in this life, figuring out what they would do to fulfill their own hopes and dreams.

I spent time emailing friends and family and becoming more computer literate, with the help of my daughter, downloading family photos on line and even playing some internet games.

I'd always been a lover of the Scrabble board game and thought that it might be fun if I were to download an Internet Scrabble game that I had stumbled upon.

And it was really fun. I was fascinated to know that I could play Scrabble with people from all over the world. You can actually chat with people as you play the game with them and it was so interesting to be able to ask different players where they were from and what they did for a living. Once you play someone on Scrabble, you can put them on a buddy list and play them again on another day if they happen to be on at the same time as you.

Well, on July 18 of last year, on my birthday, I happened to play Scrabble with a man who told me his name was Eddie. He asked me my name and I told him my name was Karen. He told me he was a New York City Policeman and we gave each other a bit of a description of what we each looked like.

I'd never done anything like this in my life. I realize now just how lonely and unhappy I was then. I was starved for attention.

I typed on the chat board, "I am about forty five years old, and I have blonde hair and brown eyes. I'm about five foot five and my look, I'd say, is that of a cross between Britney Spears and Madonna." I laughed out loud in front of my computer as I typed.

He replied, "I'm around fifty years old, I have a bit of gray hair in the temples and very blue eyes. I'm about six foot two and I have dimples. People have more than once mistaken me for Tom Selleck."

Well, his description intrigued me to say the least!

We seemed to be equal competitors at the game so after playing we agreed to put each other on our buddy lists. I had mentioned to him that it was my birthday and I have to admit I was a bit forward. I gave him an email address where he could write me if he wanted to and he gave me his.

It seemed harmless really. He lived all the way in New York, and I lived in a suburb of Chicago.

I didn't really give it much thought again until, a couple of days later, I got an email from Eddie. It was a "Happy Birthday" greeting to me. He said that he'd been busy with work but had felt bad that he hadn't really wished me well on my birthday as he should have. It was a big glittery thing on the screen, beautiful blue sparkling letters. I remember thinking how nice it was of him to do that for a virtual stranger and I thought that he must be a kind and thoughtful man.

I emailed back to Eddie and teased him a bit saying that after we had played Scrabble, I figured he had forgotten about me because I had not heard from him sooner, and how sweet I thought it was that he remembered my birthday the way that he did.

When he emailed back to me, he said, "Are you kidding? As soon as you described yourself to me that last time we chatted at Scrabble, I was hooked, you seemed so nice, and I want to get to know you better."

I felt like I had gained a new and kind friend.

And so our story began……..we played Scrabble together and we emailed back and forth every day, several times, and after just a week or so I decided to phone him which we had talked about doing, both of us curious to hear what the other sounded like. I was very cautious. I remember taking a drive to a shopping center parking lot so that I would have privacy and no interruptions.

My fingers trembled just a bit and my heart raced as I dialed his number. I could hardly believe that I was doing what I was doing, it was just so unlike me. It was totally out of character for me to be doing such a thing.

I dialed in a code before his phone number so that he would not be readily able to see my phone number on his phone.

My voice quivered as I said, "Hello."

Eddie said, "Hello to you."

Oh my goodness, his voice was so sexy, deep and a bit gravely, and he had the cutest New York accent. I teased him about his and he teased me about what he thought was an accent on my part too, which I denied as we both laughed together.

Right away Eddie started to talk about his work.

He said, "From the time I was a kid, I admired my dad who was a policeman and all his policeman friends. They were my heroes and I wanted to be just like them. My mom was a cop as well. In fact she moved up higher in the ranks than my dad and I both."

As I listened to him, I could hear the admiration in his voice, it was so endearing.

I told Eddie, "My family means so much to me and I can hear in your voice that you feel the same way, I like that."

"I like that you do, and I just love the way you say it with that funny Chicago accent," he laughed.

The conversation between us was so easy.

I laughed when he told me, "All my friends at the precinct have nicknames for all of our work buddies, guess what mine is."

"I have no idea."

"They call me EASY because I'm so laid back."

I was so not used to a man whose attitude was easy, it was refreshing to hear.

We talked that first time for about half an hour. We both had to get back to our own realities, so we said our goodbyes and talked about when we might speak next, both on line and on the phone.

We communicated every day, whether it was through email or phone conversation or texting. After another week or so, Eddie was curious to see what I looked like so I emailed a picture to him. I picked the one where I was sitting on my front porch with my legs crossed in front of me. I was wearing a rather short black and white dress and you could see that my hair was curled and kind of blowing a bit in the summer breeze.

He emailed, "Oh My God, you are such a beautiful woman, I feel so lucky to have met you."

I told him, "OK, it's your turn. You send me a picture of yourself now."

He seemed hesitant which I didn't really think too much about because quite honestly, at that point, I never thought that the friendship that we had started would develop into much of anything more than just that, because his life was in New York and mine was in Chicago.

It seemed like every day though, we found more time to speak to each other. Eddie's shift was three to midnight and I had been laid off of my job and was in the process of job hunting. Eddie and I would talk on the phone while David was at work and my kids were out of the house, at their college classes or at their jobs. We began to talk for hours, finding such comfort in each other. I began to learn more about him. In fact, after we had spoken for a few weeks, Eddie decided to change his cell phone company so that we could speak as much as we wanted to with no concern over our phone bills sky rocketing.

Sometimes at the end of the day, I would look at myself and at first wonder why my makeup was smeared, and then realize that it was because Eddie and I had laughed so much that I cried!

By this point, David and I were living such separate lives, that he didn't even notice that I was distracted by something else. He never could see beyond himself.

When I couldn't be on the computer with Eddie or on the phone talking to him, we would be texting each other. I'd keep my phone on silent and leave it in another room and then go text him and read his texts so that no one at home would notice.

Eddie finally sent me a picture of himself; he was leaning into a golf cart, golf being one of his favorite things to do, to escape, to take him away from the loneliness at home. When I looked at the picture, I noticed the note that he had sent along with it.

It said, "Nice knowing you, You probably don't want to continue our friendship now that you've seen me," which I thought was hysterical because all I saw in the photo was a middle aged man with a bit of grey hair, a wonderfully warm smile, big blue eyes and the cutest dimples. I absolutely wanted to continue our friendship.

We would meet at Scrabble and play as often as we could. Just a few weeks later, I got a surprising email from Eddie.

He wrote, "Although we have only recently met and have just been speaking for a matter of weeks, I have very strong feelings for you, feelings that feel like love."

I was a bit shaken and I thought what the hell??? How could he possibly be feeling these kinds of feelings when we had only been communicating for a few short weeks? We had never met in person! It frightened me just a bit, but again I thought it was harmless because he was in New York and I was in Chicago.

I emailed back and wrote, "You are right, we have just met and started a friendship. Let's just enjoy, for now, the conversations that we have and this new relationship. Let's go slowly, ok?"

I thought to myself that I could never feel this kind of love for someone with whom I had never met, face to face. I felt compelled to continue our friendship though; there was something about Eddie, something about the kindness in his voice.

Eddie and I began to talk about our lives as they were.

I described to Eddie what my marriage was like and he described his. He was married to the same woman, Margaret, for longer than I was married to David.

For at least a dozen years though, he and Margaret lived separate lives. He went to his job, she went to hers. She went out with her girlfriends occasionally and most nights sat in her bedroom and watched old movies alone. The only time that Eddie socialized was when he played golf in the summer with his friends or watched football in the winter with the guys. When football was over on Monday night, Eddie felt like it took forever for the next Sunday night game. Time was dragging by, he was so lonely.

Their sex lives had totally diminished about a dozen years before, when he was one day, for the one-hundredth time, so incredibly disappointed with her bored and "Are you done yet?" attitude in the bedroom. He walked out of the bedroom finally that day, never to return. She stayed in the upstairs bedroom and he stayed in the downstairs bedroom. There were many days in which there were no words spoken between them. There were days that the only form of communication between them was written down in notes to each other, only describing briefly whatever business had to be taken care of. He described the two of them to me as just two ships passing in the night.

Eddie did try several times to bring back the spark between them. He wrote her half a dozen love letters, trying to re-ignite whatever they originally had, and when he was totally ignored, he realized that their marriage was over. Eddie figured that his sex life was over too; not only with Margaret, but with any woman and so he stayed because he thought he had no other option.

Margaret was a very domineering woman who tried to control all of her family members. She would oftentimes put Eddie down, criticize him in front of family members and humiliate him. Everyone noticed it. He'd lived that way for a long time and hated it but again, he thought there was no other option, thought he was stuck.

He thought that in his middle age of life, this was as good as it gets. They both had good incomes, a roof over their heads and food to eat. They were financially comfortable. They never had any kind of violent arguments; Eddie wasn't capable of that kind of behavior.

When the two of them would go to family functions on his side, Margaret never wanted to stay long but it was quite the opposite when they went to her family's get-togethers. Eddie finally had enough of that and decided that from then on, they would take two cars wherever they went and they could each leave whenever they wanted to, without affecting the other.

Oh, we become such good actors in a dysfunctional marriage. We put on smiles when we feel like crying. We think that no one notices but they do.

Eddie had two grown children, one grandchild and a second one on the way.

We had so many things in common; he was just a few years ahead of me. We seemed to have lived parallel lives.

Through all of Eddie's unhappiness, he never expressed anger towards Margaret. He felt sorrow that things had gone wrong, never really blaming anyone, just saying that the love they had just faded away until there was nothing left. His kindness was so endearing to me.

As the days passed and Eddie and I got to know each other better, we shared stories of our lives, our work and our children. His father had died a few years before and when Eddie told me the circumstances surrounding his father's death, I could hear him get emotional. His father went into the hospital for a routine procedure and while he was there, he contracted a staph infection that led to his death. It just about killed Eddie. His dad was his hero.

I told him about my mother whom I had lost to cancer shortly after I married, way before her time. Both of us were with our parents when they took their last breaths. You just don't know what it's like to lose a parent unless you've gone through that yourself. When my mother died, I can remember thinking that I couldn't possibly face other people and continue on with my life, so I knew exactly how Eddie felt. We began to feel an incredible bond between us, something I had not experienced before. I couldn't believe that we'd only known each other for a month or so. I tried to deny what I thought I might be feeling for Eddie because it couldn't be possible, could it? How could I be feeling so strongly for this man whom I had never met face to face?

And then the subject came up, about six weeks after we had first played Scrabble together. Eddie wanted to come and meet me. It's funny because even though we were starting to feel something for each other, I never thought that he would ever come all the way to Chicago to see me. I was almost a thousand miles away. We even looked at a map online that computed exactly how many miles were between us.

I told him, "Sure, you can come and see me," thinking for certain that there was no way that he would!

We were both still married, even if just on paper. Were we crazy? It's funny now because I realize that I was, in fact, a bit crazy at that point in my life, doing some things I'd never done before and things that I never thought that I would.

It was just about one year before when I got my first tattoo! Me! A middle-aged woman getting a tattoo! I can remember walking into the tattoo parlor and just laughing my ass off wondering what in the world I was doing there in the first place as I got the tattoo!!!

It was a tattoo of my mother's favorite flower, a pink peony, on the outside of my ankle with initials signifying the bond that I had with my sister. Before I met Eddie, I actually got a second tattoo on my right back shoulder; it's a star with my grandson's initials in it. I love my tattoos. They are a part of who I am and they signify my making some major changes in my life, having the courage to do some things that I never thought that I could.

The first time that I had it done, I told no one beforehand except for my sister. When David realized that I had gotten my first tattoo, he thought I was nuts. Everyone who thought they knew me was shocked, especially my children; some of them trying to wipe it off, not believing that I would do such a thing. It was not expected of me. Everyone thought I was old reliable Karen, just doing the normal things, not making waves and just accepting all the crap around me.

I had decided a couple of years before in my mind that life was way too short to have regrets and I wanted to do things I'd never done before. I started making myself a mental list of things that I wanted to experience in this lifetime, a "bucket list" of sorts. Getting a tattoo was on my list and so were things like white water rafting, jumping out of an airplane, with a parachute of course, and hiking down the Grand Canyon.

Agreeing to let Eddie come and see me was daring on my part and again, I told no one about my plan. I felt so compelled to meet him in person. I was still surprised though when Eddie told me that he had actually purchased airline tickets to come and see me, spend one night in town and go back to New York the following day. I can remember going about my daily routine in almost a surreal like state for a couple of weeks before he actually came to see me. I still can't believe that he did or that I had the nerve to meet him!

T H R E E

I WOKE UP ON September 10, thinking I must surely have lost my mind. As I went through my morning routine of making coffee for David, making his lunch for work and cleaning up my kitchen, I was keenly aware of the fact that Eddie had already left his home in Long Island, New York and was heading for his nearby airport to take a flight to come and see me in Chicago.

After David left for work and as I jumped into the shower, I knew that Eddie was on the plane, on his way to my local airport. I had told no one of what I had planned to do that day.

When Eddie and I had first spoken about his visit, he said, "Pick out one of your favorite restaurants and I will meet you there, I want you to feel safe. I will rent a car and drive from the airport."

As crazy as it sounds it was me who said, "You don't need to do that, I will pick you up myself!"

When that morning finally arrived, there was a part of me that realized that what I was doing might be risky, but there was a bigger part of me that just didn't care. There was just something about what I had been hearing in Eddie's voice that compelled me to go ahead and just pick him up myself. I could hardly wait to see him!

It was a beautiful September morning, sunny and warm.

I took much time and care getting myself ready. I wanted to look and feel my best. I remember what I was wearing. I wore my favorite jean skirt with a grey Henley, and a pink camisole that showed atop the open buttons. It showed just a bit of cleavage. I wore my favorite sandals and gold ankle bracelet and my favorite perfume. My hair and makeup were just right too.

You know my mother always told me, "You should always look your best Karen because you never know who you might meet." She was so right.

I hopped into my car and headed to the airport with the radio playing some of my favorite music. As of late I'd been listening to some pretty funky music... very loudly! It helped to take my mind off of all the crap I was dealing with at home. I was feeling so beaten up mentally; I was exhausted with it all. I was enjoying songs that were rebellious, songs where the woman was on top for a change! My favorite song at the time talked about doing whatever it takes to be happy, no matter how unexpected. It said to dance and to love and to laugh until you cry if it makes you feel better. It said that life is too short to have regrets and to live every day to the fullest.

Such wise simple words were never truer.

I had a forty-five minute ride to the airport and never once did I think about turning back the other way. Shortly before I arrived at the airport, my phone rang and it was Eddie.

He said, "I'm here beautiful, I've got my luggage already and I'm ready for you to pick me up!"

My heart was pounding! I was so excited and nervous.

I said, "I'm just a few minutes away, I can't wait to see you!"

We stayed on the phone until I saw him standing on the crowded driveway. I actually had to pass the arrival area to turn into the airport driveway and was so delighted when I realized that I could see him standing there, from across the street; he was so tall! As I drove up to him, all I could see in the sunshine was Eddie and his dimples and his huge smile! He was very tall with huge shoulders.........and he was wearing a suit! Can you imagine? In this day and age, Eddie had decided to wear a suit to impress......and he did. The suit was my first clue to the old-fashioned romantic that Eddie was and is. He looked so handsome.... and that smile, I can remember that moment so vividly.

Eddie opened up the back door of my car and leaned in to put his suitcase on the floor of the car.

I said, "Hi Eddie."

"Hi Karen."

As he put his suitcase down, he looked at me and froze. He just stood there staring at me. He later told me that he felt like a "deer in headlights."

I laughed and I removed my sunglasses, the ones with the little pink hearts on each side, and I said to him, "Eddie, you can get in the car now."

And as if shaking himself out of a trance, he closed the back door and got into the front passenger seat next to me. We looked at each other and smiled and promptly drove out of the area, as it goes at airports, especially nowadays.

Now that he was in the car, for a moment I was shocked at having picked him up at all. It was then, for just a moment, I thought about my physical safety. This man was huge! For just a moment I thought that he could have done anything to me, I wouldn't have had a chance, but then the moment passed. As quickly as it came, it passed. Eddie sat next to me with his hands open flat on each of his knees, so as not to intimidate me. He acted like the perfect gentleman as he looked over at me and smiled.

I said, "Oh My God, I can't even believe that you are here Eddie, I am so happy to see you."

"I feel the same way Karen, you are even more beautiful than I imagined, I am such a lucky man to have met you."

As we drove away from the airport, I could feel him gazing at me.

"I feel like I'm in a dream, I can't believe that I am here," he said.

"It feels so wonderful to have you here right now, I feel like I'm meeting my best friend for the first time," I said.

I had not thought this whole day out in entirety, in fact not at all. I was trying to figure out where I was going to drive my car, where our next destination would be. Heading back in the general direction of the hotel Eddie had decided to stay at for the night, we came across a park. In fact it was the park where I used to take my kids. It was a school day and there were no kids around; so we headed for the park.

My legs were a little bit shaky as we walked up the path to the park. I was so nervous but at the same time I felt safe and comfortable next to him.

As we walked, I noticed just how tall Eddie was. He must have been a foot taller than me. He was wearing black patent leather shoes. I could smell his cologne. He smelled wonderful.

We sat down at a park bench.

Eddie said, "I can hardly believe that I'm here. I've been looking forward to this moment for so long."

"I know exactly how you feel," I said as I smiled at him.

I couldn't help staring at him as he spoke about his flight and how anxious he was to land in Chicago.

He laughed as he said, "I could hardly sit still. I kept looking at my watch. It felt like the longest flight I've ever taken!"

His laugh was so contagious and so cute and sexy. We laughed out loud together and then we just stared at each other.

This had to be the most surreal moment of my life so far. We had talked about so many things on the phone in general, and many very private things. It had been so comfortable to do so. I'd been pouring my heart out to this man for six weeks and now for the first time, I was looking into his eyes. I was taking him all in. I was connecting the voice I'd found such comfort in with all the facial features. We didn't say anything for a few minutes. We just looked at each other.

Yes, I checked him out entirely, from his hair to his suit, shirt and tie, and of course that smile of his and his dimples. I noticed the way one side of his lips curls up a bit sooner than the other when he first begins to smile. Now too, I could see the kindness in his eyes that until now I'd only been able to hear in his voice.

As I looked into those beautiful blue eyes of his, I was drinking him in; I was digesting him. As he sat next to me, I crossed my legs and I could see how he looked at me with desire. There was, without a doubt such intense electricity between us.

For just a moment, I thought that he was going to touch my bare knee and then I could see that he stopped himself. He had such self-control.

And then without warning, I just moved a little closer to him and kissed him on the lips ever so gently. It surprised us both. It brought unexpected tears to my eyes. It felt so wonderful and warm and loving. Eddie had tears in his eyes too.

We just held there for several moments, our faces touching. That moment still makes me sigh and brings tears to my eyes.

The side of the park where we were sitting became a bit cool and I said, "Do you mind if we go sit on the other side there where it's sunny and warm, I'm a bit chilly."

"Of course, that's fine." he said.

He walked behind me as we headed for the other table, and stopped me in my tracks when he took the liberty of touching the back of my neck and shoulders. For just a moment, he massaged the top of my shoulders and my neck, as he said in the kindest whisper, "Is that okay?"

"Yes, that's nice," I said.

He took the liberty then of kissing my neck from behind me. It felt so warm and wonderful. He turned me around to look at him then and he wrapped his huge arms around me and kissed me gently. Oh my goodness, I thought my heart would burst out of my chest.

Such tenderness in a kiss, I'd never known. This huge man couldn't have been more gentle and kind.

We spent another hour at the park, talking like we'd known each other for much longer than six weeks. We talked about everything.

Eddie wanted to check into the hotel, so we got back in the car and drove there.

Eddie said, "You can wait down here in the lobby or in the car if you like, I don't want you to feel uncomfortable, I'll just check in and then we can decide what to do next."

I felt safe with him and I said, "I'll go up with you. There are a lot of people around and if I need to I can always scream my head off for help. I have quite a set of lungs! Don't make me use them," I said as I looked at him with a grin.

We laughed; it just felt so comfortable and calm to be with him. It felt like such a relief to be with him now, so right.

I had just a couple of hours before I would have to say goodbye. David would be home soon and I needed to get there before him.

It felt so foreign for me to be going up the elevator with Eddie to his room. I almost felt like I was looking at us both from outside my body. I had never ever pictured myself doing what I was doing that day. We looked around the room and then we sat down and talked.

"You are the most beautiful woman I have ever seen," Eddie said.

"Thank you, you are very sweet."

He was sitting on a chair at the end of the bed where I had plopped myself down. I kicked my shoes off and sat back; I just felt so relaxed with him.

As he sat at the foot of the bed, he asked, "Would you like a foot massage?"

"Yes, I said, that would be lovely."

An hour or so went by and we talked about what we might do the next day when I came back to see him.

As I was feeling more and more relaxed, Eddie picked up his chair and moved it to the side of the bed where I was laying.

He asked, "Would it be okay if I kissed you?"

"Yes," I said.

He bent over to touch me; his kisses were so tender and warm. His lips were soft as his tongue began to explore mine. His hands began to touch my shoulders and my neck and then up to my face as he kissed me. It had been so long since I had been touched with such warmth and desire. We gave into the passion that we were feeling for each other. His hand touched my knee and started to slide slowly up my leg when there was a knock at the door.

It was the maid. It startled us so badly that Eddie jumped up and ran to the door.

He spoke to the maid for a moment and when he came back to me I realized that it was time for me to go.

He asked me, "Are you really sure that you want to come back to see me tomorrow?"

"Are you kidding? I will be back in the morning as soon as I can get out of the house," I said.

Eddie said, "I won't be able to think about anything else. Please call me when you are on your way."

"I will."

He walked with me downstairs and out to my car.

I kissed him on the cheek and promised again that I would return the next day.

As I got into my car to go home, I wondered what might have happened in the room had it not been for the maid's knock at the door.

As I drove home, my mind was filled with every detail from earlier in the day, every moment with Eddie.

I showered when I got home that day and went down to the kitchen to prepare dinner for David as was expected of me. I could never have imagined that I could do what I'd done that day and yet feel so comfortable and calm just going through my evening rituals. I believe now that it was because I knew my life with David was really over. I was just going through the motions until I could figure out how in the world I could end this marriage. I was waiting for the moment when I would be sure that I would have the courage to do what I knew would be difficult, to say the least, after all these years.

At this point, having met Eddie had nothing to do with my being sure that my marriage was over. What I was just beginning to know though, was that it felt good to be treated with respect and kindness.

No matter what happened with Eddie from this day forward didn't really matter as much as the fact that his kindness had just shown me how I should be treated. I would always be grateful to Eddie for that.

I wondered if I would chicken out and talk myself out of it again, like I had so many times before. I'd been raised with the belief that once you marry, especially in the Catholic Church, you are married for life, come hell or high water! Divorce just seemed like an impossible option.

Once again, like so many times before, after having dinner with David, we sat out on the patio in our yard and he told me what a bad day he'd had at work. In the current economic times, I was just grateful that David had a job at all. I was still job hunting after being laid off from my job. I tried to tell him once again, like so many times before, that we had to look at the good things in our life. He couldn't see it; he never could. It was becoming exhausting to try to cheer him up, to motivate him to go on another day without being miserable. It was getting more and more depressing to be with him. I thought I might explode from the frustration and unhappiness I felt when I was with him.

I felt like I had to find a way to save myself, I was losing me.

That evening, as David sat on the couch in his own miserable world, I went back and forth up to my room where I had my phone hidden and checked for text messages from Eddie, who was all alone in his hotel room. We texted back and forth a dozen times that night.

He texted, "I'm staring up at the ceiling tiles as I think about you and our visit today, I'm feeling so lonely for you. I can't eat and I can't sleep. All I can think of is your returning to see me tomorrow. Please don't change your mind. Please come back and see me."

I replied, "I can't think about anything else, I will see you tomorrow as soon as I can get away."

The next morning, like the one previous, I saw David off to work and began to prepare for my time with Eddie. It would be the last few hours that I could spend with him before he would get on the airplane back to New York. I didn't really know if I would ever see Eddie again.

When I arrived at the hotel, I called Eddie on my cell, up to his, "I'm here handsome, let me in."

When I tapped on his door, he was there immediately, with a huge smile on his face.

He had tears in his eyes as he said, "I didn't really know if you'd come back, I'm so happy you are here."

He put his arm around me and closed the door behind us. He then wrapped me in his embrace as he gently pushed me up against the wall to hold me closer. It took my breath away and I remember as he held me in his arms, I placed my foot on top of his, trying to get closer to him. I felt so safe in his arms, so content.

Eddie kissed me then, it was so warm and wonderful. His hands slid down my back as he pulled me even closer. His hands pressed up against the small of my back, drawing me closer to him. It made my body tingle all over; made me a little dizzy. His lips were soft and warm as they parted to taste me. His huge hands slid up and down my sides, his fingers just barely grazing the sides of my breasts as his fingers moved. I felt so desired like never before. We stopped for a moment and just looked up at each other and smiled. Eddie had more self-control than I did that day. I know now that he didn't want to blow it with me. He already knew that he had every intention of coming back to see me again, if I would allow him.

He didn't want to scare me with the incredible passion that he was feeling for me.

We sat down then and talked about how we'd like to spend the rest of our time together. We only had a few hours.

Eddie said, "Pick out your favorite restaurant; I want to treat you to a nice lunch."

"Okay," I said, "Let's go!"

As we walked to the car, I could feel his eyes on me; he had such a way of looking at me. He looked like he wanted to devour me. He walked ahead of me to open and close the car door for me. I got the feeling that this was the way he always treated a woman, he was not just trying to impress. It made sense to me because of the way he had always spoken to me with respect and kindness.

As we walked into the restaurant, the hostess greeted us and as she started to show us where we could sit, Eddie asked her for a table in the back corner.

When we sat down, I looked across the table at him and couldn't help but smile.

Both of us, at the same time, started to say the same thing. "I can't believe that you are really here."

It was the first of many, many times that Eddie and I would have the same thought at the same time. It was like we were meant to be exactly where we were at that exact moment in time.

We talked about our situations at home. I began to tell Eddie more about the rough times I had gone through with David. As I did, Eddie's eyes welled up with as many tears as my own. He had such genuine concern for me.

"I can't believe that any man would treat you so thoughtlessly, he's a fool," Eddie said.

I had grown so accustomed to the mis- treatment from David. Eddie's shock from how I was treated made me realize more and more that I deserved better. I deserved to be happy.

Eddie too, began to share more of what his life was like back in New York.

He said, "I figured at my age, this is as good as life gets. I assumed that I would be lonely and sad for the rest of my life. I never dreamed that I could have another chance at a happy life with someone else. And now I've met you. Maybe you would let me come back and visit you again?"

I said, "I will certainly think about it."

All the while inside myself I was screaming yes!

After we had placed our order for food and drinks, I said out loud, "I need a glass of water."

With no hesitation, Eddie called the waitress over and asked her to get that for me. I was as surprised as Eddie when his gesture brought me to tears. I had been so used to being treated in a totally different way. David pretty much looked out for himself and let me take care of myself. He never would have called the waitress over for something as simple as my need. I was so genuinely touched by Eddie's kindness.

Eddie was shocked that I had become so emotional.

"It's just a glass of water, Karen, why are you so upset?"

"I'm just not used to being treated so kindly."

Eddie shook his head in disbelief.

I realize that to someone else, Eddie's request of the waitress was not significant, but you'd have to have been living my life to understand how much it meant to me. I had met Eddie at a very crucial time in my life. I was so ready for a kind person to come my way.

As we talked, I drank my favorite Apple martini and Eddie drank beer. As our conversation continued, we laughed a lot. We laughed so hard that we cried and I got very fresh with Eddie! His eyes just about bulged out of his head when I slipped off one of my sandals under the table and slid my bare foot up his leg. His reaction made me laugh even harder; our laughter made us both feel so much more familiar with each other. It was such an incredible and welcome release!

"Look at those people across the room," I said. "They are watching us."

Eddie said, "You're right, I think they are jealous!"

We couldn't help but notice that people were looking at us. They were looking at us because we were having so much fun together! We were laughing so hard together. It was liberating to just let loose!

I just felt so good when I was with Eddie. For so long, I realize now that I was a good actress. I put on a happy face when I was in reality, feeling such turmoil inside. I was so incredibly sad with David. I didn't feel like I could be myself. I was always on guard. I was always waiting for the next shoe to drop; waiting for the next upset which I knew would arrive without question.

With Eddie now, I felt like I could be real. I could just be myself!

We sat and talked for another hour or so when we both realized that our time together was coming to a close.

I can hardly believe how anxious I felt then, as the time for Eddie to leave drew near. As I write this now, I'm crying because I can remember how I felt like it was just yesterday when we had to say goodbye. I could see by the look on Eddie's face that he was feeling the same angst.

Eddie paid the bill and then on our way out, we asked the hostess if she could take a couple of pictures of Eddie and me together. Eddie had brought his camera. She was happy to oblige. Our smiles were huge; Eddie promised to email me copies.

Eddie's arm was around me as we walked to the car. He opened the door for me and walked to his side of the car with a bounce in his step that I had not seen before.

I had to get home soon and the time of Eddie's flight did not allow me to take him back to the airport so I needed to drop him back at the hotel, where he would call for a cab. I was dreading leaving him there. So was he.

We got back to the hotel and just decided to chat in the car until the last moment that I could head back home before David got there so that I could regain my composure and deal with him while feeling sad at Eddie's departure.

"I am so happy that you came to see me Eddie. I so enjoyed our visit," I said.

"I've had a wonderful time too," Eddie said, "and if you'll let me, I'd like to come back to see you again in a few weeks."

"I promise that I will think about it. All of this is so overwhelming to me."

I knew that I was feeling the same emotion that Eddie was, but I was afraid to say it out loud just yet. I'd never been able to trust David with everything that was inside of me and there was certainly a big part of me that could not trust Eddie just yet. He needed to prove himself to me over and over again to convince me of his sincerity. I'd been hurt too much in the past.

I could hardly even speak to him much more then because I had this huge lump in my throat. I was afraid that I would cry if we were to continue the conversation.

But the time came when I had to say goodbye to Eddie. I can't believe how hard it was, after just meeting him in person for the first time. As Eddie kissed me goodbye, we both had tears in our eyes. I couldn't give in entirely to the emotion that I was feeling because I knew that I had to get home to David. I knew that I had to keep myself together. I thought that I must be nuts to be feeling what I was feeling for Eddie.

I drove up to the entrance of the hotel. Eddie turned to me to kiss me one more time and to give me a big hug, and then he stepped out of the car. He stood in the hotel driveway, paralyzed, as he watched me put the car into drive. I will never forget the lonely look on his face. The only reason that I could pull away was because I feared what could happen at home if I were not there at the expected time when David arrived home from work. So without really knowing if I would ever see Eddie again, I pulled away from the hotel. As I waved to Eddie, I looked in my rearview mirror and saw that he had not moved. He was in the exact same spot, looking at me in my car, with that same sad look on his face.

F O U R

I T'S NOT SURPRISING THAT David never suspected anything wrong with me. He never noticed that I was preoccupied with my thoughts or with anything else. He never noticed anything about me. David was always so immersed in himself; that he could never really see beyond that.

After having met Eddie face to face though, I realized that my life was never going to be the same again. It felt wonderful to be treated with such respect and tenderness.

Eddie had returned to his life in New York and I had returned to mine here.

We played Scrabble together every day. We talked on the phone for hours at a time and we texted back and forth to each other constantly. We kept realizing how many things we had in common. Some of the similarities seemed remarkable.

We did differ a bit on our music preference. While we both found such escape in getting lost in our favorite music, Eddie's first choice was old romantic tunes. He loved Frank Sinatra's music. In fact, earlier in his career as a policeman, he was a Security Officer for Mr. Sinatra while he filmed a movie in New York City.

I, on the other hand, loved all music—new and old. I shocked Eddie some of the time with the tunes that I listened to. It made me laugh to see his reaction. We exchanged titles and artists as we spoke and as we both listened to each other's music on the computer, we chose some of our favorites. One of the first songs that we enjoyed talked about a distance between two lovers. The song talks about somehow getting to each other, no matter what that means. It didn't matter if it were on a train or a plane or a bike or on the "wings of a butterfly" for that matter. We talked often about how significant the words to that song were.

More than once, as we spoke, with hundreds of miles between us, Eddie in his car and me in mine, a butterfly would land on one of our windshields or both, to our astonishment. The butterfly became a significant symbol to us. The appearance of a butterfly tugged at our heart strings whether we were together or not.

That tune became one of "Our Songs."

So many things between us seemed like they could not just be coincidence but rather fate. Fate seemed to draw us together more and more every day.

About a week after Eddie had returned to New York, he emailed me and asked if he could return to Chicago soon to see me. He had been checking prices on airfare and wanted to book his next trip to see me. Did I dare to imagine that this "thing" between Eddie and I could actually work out with so many miles between us?

I couldn't resist. We agreed on the dates; he decided to stay for two nights this time. He booked his airfare and then unbeknownst to me, he started looking around online at other local hotels. He stumbled upon a very romantic looking place that was just far enough from my home to be discreet. We talked about the possibility of staying there and I agreed to go ahead and look at the place on my own to see if I liked it. I was talking to Eddie on the phone as the hotel manager showed me the different rooms. It was a beautiful and romantic place. When Eddie asked me if it was okay for him to secure a room there for two nights, I agreed. At the time, I didn't know how many changes were about to take place in my life.

I never knew as the hours in each day passed, what might set David off. The simplest thing that might go wrong in his day was enough to make him act insanely. David went golfing one Sunday afternoon, while I was at home working around the house. My kids were all out of the house for the day. As I was preparing dinner for David and me, he came home.

I could tell the instant that he walked in the door, that there was a problem. Like so many times before, David slammed the door behind himself as he came in; so hard that the pictures that were hung on the wall shook. As he stormed into the kitchen, like so many times before, he threw his car keys violently in my direction. They hit the refrigerator door, leaving a new dent.

Like so many times before, he started screaming at me. Like so many times before, my heart sank with dread. I got this terrible feeling in the pit of my stomach, just like I always did when David would have one of his fits of rage.

When I dared to ask him what was wrong, he just got angrier……..like so many times before.

"I golfed like fucking crap again!" he screamed.

"My score was fucking disgusting! And on top of all that my fucking soda spilled all over the god damn car floor," he spewed through clenched teeth.

This was the kind of thing that could set David off into an uncontrollable fit of madness. As ridiculous as this may sound to a sane person, this is the kind of everyday occurrence that would make David furious and totally out of control.

And like so many times before, more times than I care to remember, David glared at me as he moved closer to me and yelled in my face, "I've had it! I hate my fucking life and everything in it! I'm done with you and everything else! We are selling this fucking house and I want a fucking divorce!"

I don't think he realized or for that matter cared that he had spit in my face with every word he shouted at me. I thought my heart would pound right out of my chest!

All of a sudden, almost like a clap of thunder, it became crystal clear to me what I needed to do.

But for that moment, I was quiet. It wouldn't be safe to say anything yet. I never really got angry or yelled back at him when he was in this state. I feared for my safety if I were to do that, especially when none of the kids were around to witness what was happening; he was more dangerous alone.

So, like so many times before, I just stayed out of his way while he raged.

And with that he stormed out of the room.

I would wait until he had calmed down, but I knew exactly what I needed to do. I had never been so sure, but I would wait until it was safe.

And just once more, like so many times before, David was quiet the next morning. In fact, the normal routine for David, after one of his rages was silence. He would be silent for days at a time, refusing to talk to me. Of course, he would talk to others. In fact, no one else knew of his mental state. To others, he acted like everything was fine. He saved all his nastiness for me. I was always the recipient of his wrath.

The next morning was different though. I woke up just as certain as I had been the night before of what I needed to do. David was having coffee in the kitchen when I came down.

Very calmly, I said to him, "You know what you said yesterday about wanting a divorce and selling the house? Well, it's exactly what I want too."

He looked at me and said, "Ok."

From the moment I told him, I felt like the weight of the world had been lifted from my shoulders. I felt such incredible relief with just those few words. I had no idea what lay ahead of me but it didn't matter. I'd had enough and would accept it no longer. I couldn't do it anymore. I could not continue in the same way. I had no choice; I had to save myself, finally.

With that I walked back upstairs and was about to get in the shower a few minutes later when David came up to our room. It must have taken a few moments for him to see that I was behaving differently than I ever had before.

I was not upset, I was not crying and I was absolutely certain of my decision. Unlike David, I didn't say things carelessly. He had said so many hurtful things to me over the years. Once those nasty words passed his lips, he could never take them back. They were always there in my memory. They always came flooding back to me. They always hurt, especially when he had never done anything to try to make it up to me, he just didn't even know how. And he never cared enough to try to figure it out.

It's crazy now when I think of how entrenched in this madness I was. Every time there would be a blow up between us, I would expect an apology from him and if he just said that he was sorry, I could move on. I had to sometimes beg him to apologize. It was such a pitiful situation. I realize now that he never meant any of it; didn't have a clue of how to make amends to me.

Actions speak louder than words. In fact actions screamed at me.

I said what I meant. In thirty two years of marriage, I had never threatened him with divorce.

David asked, "Can we talk?"

I said, "Of course you can talk. It won't make any difference though, because I am done. I can't live like this anymore. I can't do this anymore."

I told David that I would be moving some of my things into the spare bedroom and that I would not be sleeping in the same room with him anymore. He looked sad but I'm certain that he thought that I would change my mind, so he went along with me.

He said, "Do what you need to do."

I thought at the time that I could stay in my home until I could figure out my next move. I didn't realize that it would happen as quickly as it did.

I have an older sister who is and always will be my best friend. We have many things in common; we talk often on the phone, almost every day. We share just about everything together; we take such comfort in each other in good times and bad. Nancy and I often laugh so hard together that we cry. I don't know what I would have done all these years without her support. I hadn't told her about Eddie yet, but I had shared a bit of what would go on in my home sometimes with David.

I never really told anyone about all the details; it was just too bizarre; it was embarrassing. I held out hope for so long that David would get better. I didn't want anyone to hold a grudge against him for his behavior towards me if he ever got better. I realize now how ridiculous that was.

As of late though, I had been expressing my unhappiness more frequently. I started to explain in detail to Nancy, the absurd behavior that was taking place in my home.

In a recent conversation with her I'd told her, "I'm so tired of being miserable and afraid and lonely in this marriage. I'm going to be happy in this lifetime. With or without him, I'm going to be happy! Life is too short to feel like this every day!!"

Nancy had replied, "Karen, if you ever need to get away from him for your safety or for whatever reason, there is a room for you at my house where you can stay and feel safe."

Her generosity brought tears to my eyes. This was just the next step in the process of preparing my mind for this huge move that I was beginning to think that I would finally be brave enough to do.

I asked her, "Are you sure that would be okay with you and your family?"

"Definitely, yes," Nancy said.

I confided in Nancy that day and told her what had happened at home.

For the next couple of days, I slept in the spare room. I even felt the need to lock the bedroom door at night. I did not want to be bothered by David.

Eddie and I spoke and he sounded rather shocked when I told him what I had done. He was so supportive though, comforting me and worrying about my welfare. He felt so helpless to protect me from so many miles away. We would text back and forth just about all night long and then he would just phone me and we would whisper to each other all night.

He'd say, "Close your eyes Karen and picture me right next to you. I'll be back in a couple of weeks, just hang on; I'll be there for you to protect you and to keep you safe."

We cried together as I could almost feel his arms around me with his love and kindness. As I lay in my bed there, I could almost feel his breath on my neck, I longed for him so much.

There was more than one time that, while I spoke to Eddie late at night, I would feel so comfortable that I actually fell asleep with my phone in my ear. It was kind of funny really; we would laugh about it afterwards.

The emotional turmoil that I was going through was exhausting. After having heard so many stories of how I'd been treated by David though, Eddie was relieved to know that I was on my way to liberating myself from the craziness.

David thought the situation was only temporary at first but after several attempts of trying to convince me otherwise, he began to realize that I was serious. It was creepy to me really the way he pleaded with me. He would hug me so tightly and stroke my hair as he did so.

David tried to tell me, "I'll go to Alcoholics Anonymous meetings to try to control my anger."

I replied, "That would be good for you to do but it won't make any difference to me, it's too late. I've waited a long time for you to get better but it hasn't happened and I have no reason to believe that you ever will. Go back to meetings for yourself, not for me."

David had made promises to me since he had become sober twenty some years earlier. He never followed through. I pleaded with him to get help for himself, but he never did. I honestly hoped that he could be happy. I honestly thought that he'd be better off without me, that maybe it would force him into taking care of himself, finally.

He pleaded with me, "Please don't leave me, please stay and if I ever blow up again, then you can leave me and divorce me."

"It's too late," I said. "I can't do this anymore."

It's odd really; that he still thought that he was in control somehow. That he would give me permission then to divorce him was bizarre.

David said, "Can you really say that you don't love me anymore?"

"I will always care about you, I've been with you for most of my life but I do not love you the way that a woman should love her husband, there are just too many hurtful things that have been said and too many hurtful things that have been done. I can never forget all that, it's too late, I'm done."

My mind was made up; I'd never been so sure of anything else in my life.

I had to save myself.

David began to make me feel so uncomfortable with his pleading. He'd never been this attentive to me even in the good times. He wanted to hug me and when he did, and as he stroked my hair, he said, "You are so beautiful, I will always love you."

It made me cry because as I thought back to the last time that he had called me beautiful, I realized that it was on our honeymoon thirty two years before! It was incredibly sad. It made me cry too because I knew that it was over. The love that I'd had for him was slowly chipped away at, all those years, until it was squashed entirely.

I had found a new job in the midst of what was happening in my life. It was a job at a hospital that I knew would take one hundred percent of my concentration. I wondered if I would be able to succeed and then realized that I had no choice; I had to succeed. I had to take care of myself.

David made it impossible for me to stay in my home; he made me feel very uncomfortable when I just wanted to be left alone.

He said, "You do whatever you have to but I'm not leaving my house. This is not what I want so you can leave if you choose to, I'm going nowhere."

I had about a week before I started my new job so I decided to take my sister Nancy up on her offer for a room at her house. I hoped that I could get settled enough in that time that I could try to clear my mind as much as possible to be able to function well with the challenge of my new job. When I told Nancy that I was coming, she could not have been more kind.

I told David, "Since you won't leave our home, then you leave me no choice, I will leave."

"Please just don't move out while I'm home," he said. "I can't watch you go, please do it while I'm at work."

I told my children what I needed to do. They were sad of course and probably a bit mad at me but they knew what I had been living. I had confided in my daughters, especially. They knew how unhappy I was. My two grown daughters were still living at home; the one had just finished college, the other struggling to do so. My kids are smart though and I knew they would be all right. In fact, I knew in my heart that once we all got through this transition time, we would be so much better off.

Very shortly after I moved out, my daughters got an apartment together. They could not tolerate their dad's behavior either.

After David left for work the next day, I packed a few things and I left. Nancy was at work when I arrived at her house. I let myself in and took my things up to my new bedroom and sighed.

I called Eddie then and we talked for hours. I felt so liberated.

I had decided to confide in Nancy. When she got home from work, we went for a long walk. And I told her everything.

As we walked, the floodgates opened. I poured my heart out to Nancy and she listened. I told her about David's absurd behavior. I told her that it had been going on for years. She asked me why I didn't tell her sooner and I went on to explain my hope that he would get better.

And then I told my sister about Eddie. She could see my face light up; she could hear the joy in my voice. She was at first shocked but then as I went on, she felt happy for me.........and concerned.

She was concerned, of course, for my safety first, and then she said, "Oh my God!! You are not thinking about moving to New York!! Are you?"

I told her that I probably would not, when in reality, I had already thought if that was what I needed to do to keep Eddie in my life, I probably would.

Nancy promised to stay quiet about the things I had told her for now. I did not know how everything would work out in any part of my life; she was the only family member I had told so far about Eddie.

I got settled into my new space in my sister's home and started my new job at the hospital and like I'd thought it was mind boggling and a bit overwhelming! It was so good for me because when I was at work, I couldn't really think about anything else. It was a good distraction from the reality of my life.

I was talking to Eddie a couple of days later when the realization hit me. I had previously thought that when Eddie came to visit, that I'd be spending a few hours each day with him and then going home to David.

I said, "Eddie, do you realize that now that I'm on my own, when you come in, I can spend as much time with you as I choose to?"

"That's true, isn't it?" he said.

"I could spend every moment with you if I want to," I said coyly. "All night long if I choose to!"

"I would love that."

All I knew then was how good it felt to be with him, to be loved by him, to be taken care of by him, to be protected by him. It made me feel wonderful!

I absolutely wanted to further explore this relationship and this connection that I felt with him.

So I began to live my life anew, it felt surreal. It felt incredible!

I worked just a few days a week. I talked with Eddie every moment that we could and I enjoyed the peacefulness that was mine now, most of the time anyway. David would call me to see what I was doing. He wanted to know who I was with and what I was doing. He seemed to care more now than he ever had before. It was such a good feeling as a bit of time went by, when I realized that I didn't even have to pick up the phone when he called if I didn't want to, and sometimes I didn't! I had been so involved with David from such a young age that it was a gradual process of letting go of everything that I had associated with him. There was so much turmoil with him. It was such a relief not to be immersed with that every day. I found that the longer that I was away from him, the more clearly that I could think. It was the beginning of the healing process.

I finally worked up the courage now that I was away from David, to file for divorce. I phoned a local lawyer and started the process. It was a difficult but necessary decision.

I was anxious to get it over with now, to detangle myself from David and all the unhappiness that I associated with him.

I got along so well with my sister and her family. They all made me feel so welcome. Not once did I ever feel like I was in their way, I'll always be grateful to them for helping me to liberate myself from the situation that I was in.

Before I knew it, it was time for Eddie's October visit. I was so excited, we both were. We had a countdown of sorts to the day that he would arrive in my town again. He sent me the sweetest emails every day, telling me how much he wanted to hold me and to kiss me and to spend time with me. I wanted the same.

F I V E

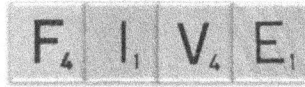

I HADN'T FELT SO light-hearted in a very long time, as I did that morning in October on my way to the airport to pick up Eddie. I felt like I must surely be living someone else's life! It felt great to wake up every morning choosing to be happy.

It was a wonderful feeling not to be exposed to enormous negativity every day.

Eddie and I had talked a lot on the phone about how anxious we were to see each other again. The anticipation for his being with me was something I'd never experienced before in my life.

In our phone conversation I said, "I can hardly wait to be with you again, just to have you stand next to me; just to touch your hand, I miss you so much."

Eddie said, "I can't wait to get my hands on you, to touch you, and to kiss you, and to hold you and to make you feel safe."

"I can't wait to look into your beautiful blue eyes again, Eddie."

I knew that I would feel safe every moment that I was with him. I knew that we would laugh and we would have wonderful conversation. I knew that I could be one hundred percent me. I could say whatever was on my mind, without being told that my feelings were stupid and not valid. I could just totally let loose. Eddie liked me no matter what.

I was so excited as I drove to the airport, singing loudly to my favorite music. I was singing the song about the "Wings of a Butterfly." I was feeling euphoric, like I'd had a few drinks! I was high on life, like never before! It was an incredible feeling! I could hardly wait to see Eddie!

Nowadays, there is much security at all the airports and they don't allow you to spend much time curbside as you drop off and pick up passengers.

I had dared Eddie on the phone, "I dare you to kiss me for so long right there on the airport driveway, so long that security yells at you to get in your car and go."

Eddie laughed at my challenge!

It became habit then for Eddie to phone me shortly before I arrived at the airport to let me know that he had landed and had his luggage and was ready for me to pick him up. We would stay on the phone until I could see his smiling face. And that smile of his, hmmm, it struck me every time, right in the pit of my heart and this day in October was no different. The weather was brisk and fall- like, I could see his breath, as I drove up to him. His blue eyes sparkled as he smiled at me. His jacket was blue too, which made his eyes look even bluer.

I got out of my car to greet him. I came around to his side of the car. We had talked in detail about exactly what we wanted to happen when we were to see each other again. We rehearsed over and over in our minds our time together. When we couldn't be together, it was all we had. The anticipation was all we had. The anticipation of our next visit and the memory of our last was what we had.

As I walked towards him, all I could see was his smile and his lips and I just crashed right into them. It was such a relief to be in his arms, no words were necessary at that moment; it brought tears to my eyes and to Eddie's too. And he kept his promise. We kissed passionately for a long time, long enough to draw attention to ourselves. Before we knew it, the security guard was yelling at us to be on our way, but we kept kissing until he got a little closer to us. We laughed then and I hopped into the car next to Eddie.

As we slowly drove out of the airport, we looked at each other and smiled.

Eddie said, "You look more beautiful now than you ever have Karen. I've missed you so badly!"

In fact, I think he told me that a dozen times in the first fifteen minutes that we were together. At every street light, we kissed and laughed and reveled in the fact that we were together, again, at last.

As soon as it was possible, we pulled over into a parking lot. We couldn't wait any longer. We both just needed to stop and look at each other, uninterrupted. That's exactly what we did. We just needed to allow our hearts to slow down a bit.

I felt such joy as I sat next to Eddie.

When I looked into his eyes that day; I knew. I knew that I was falling in love with him. Never before, did I have this overwhelming emotion inside. Never with anyone else had I felt what I was feeling now. I had no idea that the way I felt even existed. I thought my heart might burst right out of my chest!

Eddie cupped my face with his hands and kissed me ever so tenderly. Again, we were both brought to tears as we gave into our emotions. We began to refer to these moments as "emotional waves", for lack of a better explanation. It described all the times that while we were speaking or even thinking about each other, that we would be choked up with feelings for each other. Those moments were all encompassing. There was nothing else. And they happened more and more with every moment in time.

Eddie said, "Oh my God Karen, I love you so." It was then that I could hold back no longer.

"I've never felt this way before in my life Eddie; I'm falling in love with you too."

I shook my head in disbelief as I told him and as I realized just how strong my emotion was for him. It just didn't seem possible in the few weeks we had known each other. I never would have believed it if anyone else had told me they were in the same situation, just didn't think it was possible. When I had watched movies or read love stories before, I had honestly thought that it was nice but come on, those kinds of things don't really happen to people. They don't really feel so strongly for each other, do they? I was just beginning to realize that in fact, fairy tale love like that could happen! It was happening to me!

We sat in the parking lot there for about half hour before we could tear ourselves away from each other. I never would have believed before this that I could just sit next to a man and look into his eyes and touch his hand and feel so fully content.

I said, "Wait until you see this place where we are staying, it's gorgeous!"

As he laughed Eddie said, "I really don't care what it looks like, I'm just so happy that I am here with you."

Eddie moved towards me and kissed me on the side of my neck and said, "I've missed even your smell, mmm, you smell delicious."

"Thanks Eddie," I said.

Then as Eddie held my hand, we drove to our next stop.

We had decided to stop at the park where we had our first kiss which was a short distance from where we had parked. We got out of the car and sat at the same table where we had sat the first time we were there. We talked about what we might do these next few days together. Our time together was so precious; we didn't want to waste a moment.

We talked and we kissed and we talked and we held hands. Eddie wanted to know if now that I was living at my sister's place, if there was anything that I needed at the store. He wanted to take care of me.

We drove to the store and picked up some things we'd need in our room and Eddie encouraged me to get whatever I needed. I picked up some toiletries and some snacks. We stopped at a liquor store and bought what we needed to have our favorite drinks. We planned on spending lots of time alone together.

Our room was ready when we got to the hotel. It was a beautiful room with a king sized bed that was covered in rose petals. There was romantic music playing on the stereo when we arrived. In one corner of the room, beyond the fireplace, was a huge whirlpool tub and on the counter were two champagne glasses. It was a lover's wonderland.

After bringing in our luggage and getting settled in, Eddie made us drinks. He drank scotch and he made me a martini. Eddie put some romantic music on that he had brought with him. He had burned some CDs just for this occasion.

He turned to me and said, "Dance with me baby."

I smiled and said, "Of course Eddie."

Any excuse for him to hold me in his arms was good for me.

And as the music played, we danced. I had never enjoyed older romantic music as much as I did with Eddie. It was just so fitting the two of us together. We held each other tight and danced slowly as Eddie whispered in my ear.

"I love you Karen and I want to be with you always and forever."

Slow dancing with him was the best way for me to just hold him and to be close to him physically. My body was yearning for his touch. I was craving his warmth. I melted into him.

As we listened to the music, Eddie went to his bag to get a small wrapped box that he handed to me.

"I bought a little something for you Karen; I couldn't resist when I saw it. I couldn't help but think of you."

I opened it to see it was a beautiful gold necklace with a butterfly pendant on it. I started to cry because it had such significance for us. The song that we both enjoyed so much together about the "Wings of a Butterfly" was one that I listened to often. It became so important to us because of the distance between us.

I told him, "I love it; help me put it on."

It was beautiful.

Our room was dark with soft lighting and candlelight. It was the kind of place where you could just get lost in love and romance.

And we did.

As we danced that night, Eddie said, "I've thought about this moment for the last four weeks, since I had to leave you to go back to New York. I'm so happy that you allowed me to come back to see you again."

"I could hardly wait for you to get back here," I said.

"All the while I was back in New York, I thought about this moment when I could hold you in my arms again. I've dreamed about dancing with you just like this. I love you Karen."

"I love you too Eddie."

With that, Eddie and I kissed more passionately then we ever had before as we moved towards the bed. He turned me around so that I was facing the bed as he stood behind me. There were mirrors on the walls across the room in front of us so I could see as he started to kiss my neck and his arms wrapped around my waist. He ran his hands up and down the sides of my body while his fingertips just barely touched the sides of my breasts. I could feel my heart racing in anticipation of what was to come.

Eddie started to undo the buttons of my blouse, slowly, one by one. As he held me close, he smelled so good. He wrapped his hands around both my breasts as I moaned with pleasure and as I turned around to face him again, he reached around me to unclasp my bra and as it fell to the floor, he pushed me back on the bed and we got lost in each other. We had talked so many times on the phone about what this moment would be like, when we could finally be together this way.

I had pictured it in my mind so many times. The reality of the moment was beautiful.

Eddie was the most gentle and generous lover I'd ever known. He wanted to know my every desire.

Time seemed to stand still, we didn't know if it was day or night for most of the time. It was magical. We spent our time talking and dancing and kissing and making love. We made sweet passionate love. I felt like I could just be beside Eddie every day all day long.

The way that he looked at me, oh the way he looked at me; took my breath away. He looked at me like he wanted to devour me; never in my life did I feel so wanted. It made me swallow in order to catch my breath. I wanted to feel this way forever. It was so powerful what we felt for each other.

We got to know each other better that visit. Eddie told me more about himself. He told me about some of his experiences as a police officer. Every story he told me made me care for him more. You would think that a New York City police man would be really tough and I'm sure that when he needed to be he was but such a compassionate man I would have never imagined to do the job that he did.

He told me about the time he found what seemed like a homeless man on the streets of New York while walking his beat.

He told me, "The man's body seemed lifeless, slumped over on the ground. It was such a cold wintery night. As soon as I found him, I called an ambulance. It was my job then to search his body for an ID and what I found shocked me. I found thousands of dollars in cash in his pockets!"

Just the way that Eddie told me the story touched my heart. He felt such compassion for this man, wondering why he would opt to sleep on the street when, in fact, he had the cash to have stayed at a hotel. He wondered too whether or not this man had a family and what may have led up to the state that he was in now. Sadly, this man died.

Eddie told me too, that he had on more than one occasion, carried young children out of apartment complexes, as their parents were being arrested on drug charges or other crimes. Some of these children had been injured by the ones who claimed to be their family.

He said, "There were cigarette burn marks up and down this little girl's arms."

"Oh Eddie, how awful."

He had tears in his eyes as he remembered the experience like it was yesterday.

As he carried these kids out of harm's way, he said he didn't care who saw that he had tears running down his face for these poor innocent children. I had never seen such compassion in a big strong man before like his.

Eddie's stories were fascinating, he had so many to tell.

We spent the rest of that day and night, just the two of us in the hotel room. I didn't want to go anywhere, didn't want to share Eddie with anyone. I wanted him all to myself.

The passion between us was electric. We spent hours just looking into each other's eyes, never before had I realized what incredible windows to the soul that they are. It was almost like we could read each other's minds, knowing that we both felt this overwhelming love and desire for each other.

The next evening we decided to go out for dinner to a romantic supper club. While we visited, money was no object, we indulged ourselves. Eddie and I got dressed up, he looked so handsome. He was wearing a brown sports coat and a light blue shirt that made his eyes look as clear as the sky outside. And he smelled so damn good. I wore black slacks with the cutest little black boots and a sexy maroon top that was low cut and showed lots of cleavage.

Eddie was drooling before dinner.

It was a quiet, candlelit restaurant. We sat in the darkened bar area, near the piano player. Eddie had told me how proud he was to be walking beside me and as we sat there, he said quite loudly as he looked across the room at the other people there, "That's right all you people, this beautiful woman right here, she's with me!"

We laughed as we drank and ate a delicious steak dinner, all the while sitting closely and enjoying the piano music that played. The whole world could have fallen down around us and we would have continued to gaze into each other's eyes in love. There was nothing else, just the two of us, that's how it felt.

After dinner, we went back to our room and lit a fire and talked for hours, we started to talk about the possibility of a real relationship between us, and a lasting one and how that might be possible considering the distance between us.

I started the water in the whirlpool tub. I was wearing a white lacey tee shirt and little else as we sank into the tub and started kissing passionately. We were very serious until the pressure of the water pushed Eddie to the opposite end of the tub. We roared with laughter. It was just the first time, the first of many, when we would be in the throes of passion when something would strike us as funny and we would laugh so hard we would cry. And then in the next moment, we'd get serious again and fall into romantic ecstasy.

Now that Eddie's visit was coming close to ending, the two of us, without knowing for sure what the other was thinking, started to panic. Whenever I would think about him leaving, I'd feel so sad and lonely. Both of us experienced such emotional waves. We would take turns stressing at the thought of being apart again, not really knowing for sure when we could be together again.

Most often, these moments would happen to us one at a time and one of us could comfort the other. But some of the time, we both felt bad at the same time, and we'd cry together. All the while, I kept thinking this was crazy. The feelings were so extreme, it was hard to believe. At some points, our emotions were totally out of control.

I gazed into Eddie's eyes as we lay in bed together the night before he left. We held each other all night long. I felt so good when I was with him. I felt like such a woman, not a mother or a wife or a grandmother, just a desirable woman. I could have stayed right there with him forever.

We tried to avoid discussion of him leaving for as long as we could but the next morning, we both knew we needed to check out of the hotel. So we packed up the car and headed in the direction of the airport.

We stopped to have lunch at one of my favorite restaurants. Eddie drank a beer with his hamburger. I drank my favorite Appletini and we talked. Our conversations had become so intimate. As we spoke about each other's past love lives, it was funny that I found myself becoming a bit jealous. I'm smiling now as I recall how I felt. I was starting to wish that Eddie and I had met earlier in our lives and that he was all mine, always. But as we discussed it, I began to realize that if it hadn't been for all the life experiences that we had both been through, we would not be the same people that we had become. Perhaps we would not have felt for each other what we were feeling. We realized that we probably met at the most perfect time in our lives.

I told Eddie, "I think that God has played a trick on you and me; what with making us wait more than half of our lives to meet each other."

"Yes," he said, with that irresistible smile of his "but oh my, it was so worth the wait!"

Our next stop on the way to the airport was the park. It became traditional now for us to visit there at the beginning and ending of our every visit. The weather was rainy and cold, just as gloomy as I was feeling, so we didn't get out of the car. We sat next to each other and tried to have a normal conversation but it just wasn't possible because I was so distracted by the feeling of loneliness that was mine at the prospect of his leaving.

My eyes welled up with tears as I told Eddie, "I don't want you to go, and I don't know how I'll get by without you here by my side."

Eddie tried to be strong for us both.

He said, "As soon as I get back to NY, I'll look at flights to return to you for another visit in just a few weeks. I don't know how I'll get through this time but we have no choice for now until we both get some things settled."

And then he surprised me. Besides his coming back in November, Eddie asked, "Would you consider taking a trip to come and see me in NY for our December visit? I would love to treat you to some of the local sights of New York City at Christmas time!"

He wanted to share with me some of the highlights of the city. He wanted to share with me some of his hometown. The prospect of going to visit him there was exciting but a little frightening. I had never travelled on my own. I told him that I would think about it and that we would talk about it more. The thought of our next couple of visits together did help to distract me for a bit so that I was able to drop him off at the airport. We both knew that once we drove up to the airport, we had to say a quick goodbye because of the security there. We were not allowed to linger there.

We held hands up until the point where Eddie got out of the car curbside and came around to the passenger side where I sat. I got out of the car and put my arms around him as I looked up into his eyes to say goodbye. I held back the tears as well as I could as we kissed. It was a good thing that security was so tight there and that I had no choice but to leave quickly because I didn't want to cry anymore, not for Eddie to see anyway. As I drove away, I didn't look back; I couldn't. I couldn't bear to see the emotion that I knew was all over Eddie's face. And as I drove away, I told myself not to cry because if I did, I would not be able to see where I was going through the tears.

I started my drive back to my sister's place. I had a forty-five minute drive back. Within a matter of minutes, my cell phone rang and it was Eddie.

"I miss you so much already."

I could hear the loneliness in his voice. I felt exactly the same as he did. I could hardly speak.

Once I wasn't looking directly in his eyes though, it was just a little easier not to cry. Once I couldn't smell him, it was a just a little easier. Once it was no longer possible to touch him, I could bear it, just barely. We talked all the way up to the time that I arrived back at Nancy's and once Eddie knew that I was there safe, we hung up the phone for just a little while.

I got settled in back in my room. Nancy came up and we talked about my visit with Eddie. She listened as I told her how I was falling in love with him. She expressed her concern when I told her that I was considering a trip out to New York in December. My safety was her first concern. She couldn't possibly understand how I was feeling or how I could possibly be feeling so much so soon. I didn't understand how it was possible. How could she? I told her that if I was being a fool though, so be it. But there was this wonderful man offering me a free trip to New York, why not? I thought. Of course, I would go. I had decided already that I would go. No matter what happened, I'd be that much smarter for the experience.

As I lay in bed that night, I relived every moment of the last few days with Eddie in my mind. And right before I fell asleep, I got a text from him.

"I'm home my darling. I love you. Sweet dreams. I'll talk to you tomorrow."

I was emotionally exhausted and fell fast asleep.

S I X

S O EDDIE WAS BACK in New York once again and I was home alone. We went back to speaking on the phone whenever we could, texting each other all day long and longing for each other.

Longing for him was starting to become so physically painful. I could hardly eat; it was hard to think sometimes. An ache such as this I'd never known.

The days that I worked, I was up before dawn and out the door. I was busy at my job but Eddie was always on my mind. I would phone him on every break I got and as I walked to my car at the end of the day, I was phoning him again. I never knew for sure if I'd have the privacy I needed to talk with him at my sister's so I would stop in a parking lot somewhere on my way home. I knew then that I could be candid and open with him. We could talk for as long as we wanted to uninterrupted. I could laugh as loud as I wanted and I could cry if I needed to………and I did. Our love affair made me feel so emotional.

I would have a little dinner with Nancy, watch a little TV, all the while texting Eddie and then off to bed. I'd go up to my room and lock the door. As I got comfortable for the night, I phoned Eddie and we spoke while I lay in bed until I couldn't keep my eyes open any longer. Sometimes we didn't even need to speak, just so long as we were connected with a phone in each of our ears. I felt close to him that way, as close as we could be with almost nine hundred miles between us. And we talked about every detail of how we would make love again when we were together once again. It was as close to bliss as we could get without being in the same room together.

I felt so comfortable that more than once I fell asleep with the phone in my ear. I'd wake and realize what had happened and I'd see there was a text on my phone or a voicemail. Eddie was always there for me. I was beginning to feel in my heart that I could count on him, that he would never fail me. I felt so secure. I felt his warm arms around me even absent his body.

His voicemail would say, "Karen, I love you. Sweet dreams baby."

He left me voicemails if I couldn't pick up or he'd leave them on purpose when he knew that I was working and not able to listen to them right away. It was always such a nice surprise. I craved everything about him when we were apart.

His messages made my heart pound. They made me laugh and cry. I can remember sitting in the break room at work listening to them over and over again when he wasn't available for me to speak to live. I took such comfort in just hearing his sweet voice.

I saved all the messages until my phone could no longer hold any new ones. And then when I had to delete some to make room for more, I'd listen to each one carefully again and decide which ones I could possibly live without hearing again. I still have about a dozen of them.

In one he is singing to me. He is singing one of the romantic songs we first danced to in our hotel room.

He sang, "It's late in the evening, she's wondering what clothes to wear. She puts on her makeup and brushes her soft blonde hair. And then she asks me, do I look all right? And I say yes, you look wonderful tonight."

In another message he's choked up as he says, "I'm driving down the street here on Long Island and I had to pull over as I am thinking about you, listening to music on the radio. It's so painful, I'm longing for you so badly."

And in still another, he's laughing a little devilishly as he says in a low voice, "Oh yeah, in just twenty four hours from now Karen, I'll be there with you and you are all mine. I can't wait to get my hands on you."

Eddie booked his flight for our November visit. He would be here the week before Thanksgiving for three nights. We were going to stay at the same romantic place that we'd been the visit before. I couldn't wait.

The countdown began.

The days of the week were identified only by how many were left before I'd see his smiling face. I longed for his touch. I'd close my eyes and pretend he was next to me. I imagined his breath on my neck, I could almost feel it. I could almost hear him breathing as I imagined him in my bed right next to me.

We counted the days down together many times a day. When we got to seven days, we became quite frantic until we were counting the minutes until we'd once again be in each other's arms.

We'd laugh and we'd cry together in anticipation of our time together. And finally, once again, the morning of his arrival finally got here. Eddie was in the sky on his way to me. My heart soared to new heights I'd never imagined. I never felt so overcome with emotion, never knew this feeling even existed.

Everyone was out of the house or sleeping as I snuck out quietly with my suitcase.

It was so much fun really having this secret relationship. It made me smile all the way to the airport as I blasted my music and listened to my favorite song about the "Wings of a Butterfly"!

My sister was still the only one who knew where I was going to be and I told her, "If anyone asks, please tell them that I've taken a trip to Paris. I don't want to risk word getting back to my soon to be ex about my whereabouts."

It was no longer his business.

I was pulling up to the airport just as Eddie called me to let me know he was ready.

It began to feel like we had ESP. We seemed always to be on the same page in our minds. So often, we were thinking the same thing at the same time and sometimes even said those things out loud. We would laugh in disbelief when it happened.

As soon as I saw him, I thought that my heart would burst. Every time I saw Eddie, he looked more handsome to me. I jumped out of the car into his waiting arms and we both had tears in our eyes as we kissed and hugged. Once again, we got yelled at by security because we got so lost in each other's eyes and lingered too long for security's sake.

We drove past the park this time, the weather was wet. We stopped at the store for a few things essential to our time together and headed in the direction of the hotel. We stopped for some lunch, knowing full well that once we got to the room, we may not leave any time soon.

Oh my God, it was such a huge relief to be with him again. It was like I could breathe when I was with him. It felt like I'd held my breath waiting for him to arrive. It felt like I'd held my breath ever since he got on the plane last time to return to New York four weeks previous. In the restaurant, we both had a drink; it was good to calm our nerves.

I don't even remember what we ate. We just looked into each other's eyes as we spoke about how much we'd missed each other.

Eddie said, "The plane couldn't go fast enough! I thought I just might run up and down the aisle of the plane screaming!"

I laughed and said, "You poor thing, I know exactly how you feel, I've been going nuts!"

"It seemed to take so long to get here. I couldn't stop looking at my watch. I turned it around on my arm, hoping that I could stop looking at it."

"I'm so happy that you are finally here again with me."

"Me too," he said as he smiled. "Just wait until I get you alone, I'll show you just how much I've missed you."

We both laughed then.

After lunch, we checked into our romantic getaway place and we sat on the couch together and had a drink. Never in my life have I felt such contentment just gazing into someone's eyes. I could have stared at him all day long and I know that he felt the same.

Eddie put on some beautiful music then and we danced. I could feel his heartbeat, he held me so close…for a long time.

He couldn't wait any longer then; Eddie had brought gifts for me. He did such a good job of wooing me, like no other. He was so concerned for me with the frigid Chicago weather coming and wanted to be sure that I was ready and as if to keep me warm in his arms, he provided me with what I needed. He brought me a scarf for around my neck and gloves to match. He put a soft plush steering wheel cover in my car for me. If you live in a location with frigid winter weather, then you know what a blessing that can be.

And then he handed me a little box.

"This is for you, my love."

"Oh Eddie, what have you brought me this time?" I said with a little smile.

My hand went to my mouth as I gasped when I opened it. It was a beautiful gold ring with two interlocking hearts.

"That is your heart and mine." Eddie said. "We are meant to be together now and forever. Please wear this as a symbol of you and me."

As I slipped it onto my finger I said, "Thank you, it's so beautiful."

I remembered then that during his last visit, we had gone to a jewelry store and I had tried on some rings. That was how he knew the exact size to get me. I began to realize then that Eddie had a way of remembering details. He seemed to remember every little thing about me that I'd revealed thus far.

He said, "Have you thought about my offer to fly you out to New York next month for our next visit? I want to show you Manhattan at Christmastime. You will love it!"

I said, "I would love that, yes! How can I resist you?"

He held me tight then as we sat down on the bed and kissed. It felt like I was in a fantasy. This was what love should feel like I thought.

And I gave into him as he pushed me back gently onto the bed. We didn't know what time of day it became, we were so mesmerized with each other. We made love so gently and slowly and patiently. He touched me like I'd never experienced before. He traced every inch of my body so tenderly with his fingers.

"I want to memorize every single part of you so that when we can't be together, I can close my eyes and imagine that you are with me, and I can remember how you feel," he said as he lay next to me with his eyes closed.

Never before had anyone spoken to me like this, with such tenderness and sincerity.

"I love you Eddie."

This was when he began to know the most intimate things about me and what made me feel good physically.

Eddie said, "Tell me your favorite parts; show me what makes you feel best. We won't have to waste any time next time. I'll know what you enjoy the most."

I said, "It's wonderful being with you this way Eddie."

"I want to do whatever makes you happiest Karen."

I was putty in his loving hands. I'd never been with a man before who cared so much about pleasing me. I was in heaven.

It was so touching when, for the first time he noticed my incision from having my children by cesarean section. When he realized what it was, his face was overcome with emotion. He looked up at me as his eyes welled with tears when he imagined the pain I must have endured in recovering from surgery. Such compassion in a man's eyes, I'd never seen.

Each act of kindness made me feel more intimate with Eddie. He was really getting to know me inside and out. I never would have believed that such a big strong man could be so kind and compassionate and gentle. I couldn't help being drawn to him, more and more with every encounter.

Finally, we were exhausted and fell asleep in each other's arms. Hours later we knew that it was the morning only by opening the room darkening drapes to see it was sunny outside. It was wonderful to wake up next to Eddie. I'd open my eyes and he was right there next to me smiling at me. There was nothing else, just Eddie and me.

Every day and every moment with Eddie was calm and peaceful and good. He was on an even keel all the time. I'd been so used to being with someone whose behavior was manic that it seemed unusual to be with someone like Eddie. He was so totally the opposite end of the spectrum from what I was used to with David. I was always expecting him to get angry about something outside of us or at me. I began to realize how profoundly David's behavior had affected me. That I expected erratic moods from Eddie made me realize how my thinking had become distorted. Being with Eddie, I realized, gave me the clear-headedness to think more normally. It was such a huge relief!

Eddie loved me no matter what and he wanted to know everything about me. He wanted to notice when I might be moody or sad or ecstatic or whatever. He wanted to learn how to help me, how to make me feel better, both physically and mentally. He wanted to be my rock, my refuge. He wanted to know what I liked in bed………exactly……. because he wanted to please me in every way. I was not used to that. I didn't know that if a man loves you in a very intimate way that he would go through so much trouble to be there in every way.

I woke several times during the night only to reassure myself that Eddie was in reality, by my side. I thought I might just be dreaming that he was with me. I wanted nothing more than to be with him always and couldn't sleep for more than a couple of hours at a time. It became the norm for me when I was with him to wake often through the night just to hear him breathe. Only then could I fall back asleep for a while.

Our time together every time that he visited became an exquisite escape for us both. He was away from the sadness and loneliness at home and so was I.

Eddie had brought me a police uniform shirt which of course, I modeled for him much to his delight! I wore nothing else but the shirt as he snapped pictures of me so that he'd be able to remember these happy moments when we were once again apart, which we were both always so keenly aware of in the back of our minds. The time we spent together went by alarmingly fast.

Before we knew it, several days had passed and our visit came to an end. It was time to pack up our things and to drive back to the airport.

All we had to do was to look into each other's eyes to see what the other was thinking. We could hardly speak the words of our pending departure, it was too sad. We went through the motions we knew we needed to. We drove to the park after having lunch at what was becoming our favorite restaurant.

We spoke about our upcoming visit where I would visit him in New York. We both looked so forward to it.

Eddie said, "There are several things that I want to show you when you get to New York. We will stay someplace really nice but I'm not going to tell you more because I want you to be surprised, all of our plans are in the works!"

I said, "I can hardly wait."

I didn't know how I could make it through the next few weeks without him by my side. The prospect was overwhelmingly crushing. Eddie was outwardly stronger than me, emotionally.

As he hugged me and whispered in my ear how much he loved me, I couldn't hold back the tears. Eddie promised me that our December trip would be the most memorable yet and that I had to try to concentrate on that to help me get through the next month apart.

We also began to talk about our future plans together. Eddie wanted to wait until after Christmas to let his wife Margaret know that he wanted a divorce. He wanted to let her know that he would no longer settle in his life. He now knew as I did, what true love and happiness felt like and he wasn't willing anymore to settle for less. Eddie didn't want to spoil his whole family's holidays with the pending divorce and I could understand that. He wanted to allow Margaret to experience her last "family" Christmas with her children.

He was not angry at Margaret, only sad that their love had disappeared. His kindness compelled him to wait until after the holidays.

Eddie and I began to speak about how we could actually be together all the time in the same location and we talked about where we might live. In my mind, I was already thinking that I would go anywhere with him. If he wanted me to live up on a secluded mountaintop, that would be okay with me. Anywhere he wanted to live would be fine with me as long as we were together.

Eddie said, "As much as I love being on the Police Department, I've actually been considering retiring for about a year now. I've been on the fence about it weighing the pros and cons."

"Really?" I said, "But you love it."

"I do love it but I've got over twenty years in and I'm looking forward to a great pension and to doing some new things in my life."

I said, "Are you sure that's really what you want Eddie?"

He said, "You say the word and it's done, I love you and want to be with you. You can't leave your kids here. They need you more than mine need me back in NY. If you'll have me there's no doubt in my mind that now would be the perfect time for me to retire."

But even as he began to make promises to me, I had a hard time believing him. My disbelief had nothing to do with Eddie. It had everything to do with me and my mindset. I'd been so used to things in my life being bad. I'd lost all my trust in my husband and even though I knew that I was in love with Eddie, I couldn't trust one hundred percent that he would follow through with what he was telling me. I was so used to being disappointed by David. I hoped with all my heart that it was true and that all the things Eddie told me would actually happen. I couldn't help but be doubtful. So for now, I thought, I will have to be cautious.

Eddie drove us then back to the airport and we said our goodbyes.

It was heart wrenching as usual. As I drove home and Eddie phoned me when he was ready at his gate to board the plane back to his hometown, I could hear in his voice that he too was just as upset about his leaving me, he'd only been strong on the outside for my benefit, to try to help me through our farewell.

When we spoke the next day on the phone, I realized how difficult it was for him to go home to Margaret.

He said, "When I got back to the airport on Long Island, I couldn't even go home right away, it was just too depressing. I stopped at the local bar and had a couple of drinks and replayed the last few days in my mind. And then I went back to my dungeon. The only thing that will keep me going for the next few weeks will be making all our plans for when you arrive here."

"I understand, I feel the very same longing as you do Eddie."

For the next few weeks, Eddie and I talked nonstop about how much we were both looking forward to our December visit. He told me about some of the different places we would visit and some of the things that we would see. In just a few days, he had bought my airline tickets and had reserved a room at a Bayside Hotel in Port Jefferson on Long Island.

He never disappointed me. I was beginning to see that the things he promised really did come true. The things that he told me he would do, he did. I began to dare to trust him, not entirely, but it was a beginning.

All I knew is that I felt wonderful. Eddie surprised me all the time. He did everything that he could from almost nine hundred miles away to make me feel safe and loved and cherished.

I came home from work several times during that month to packages that had been delivered. Eddie was so concerned that I'd be warm enough at night and as if to mimic his warm and strong arms around me, he sent me an electric blanket. We spoke every night at bedtime and it gave him such pleasure to know that even in the midst of a cold and wintery night, I was warm and cozy as we spoke.

His goal was to make me believe in him, to believe what his intentions were.

"Please be patient with me Karen. I want nothing more in this world but to be with you but you and I both have things to deal with in our lives now. You have to deal with your divorce and I have to deal with mine."

"Yes, I know that," I said.

One evening when we spoke and I was feeling insecure without him, he asked me if I could do him a favor.

He said, "Karen, whenever you are doubtful of me, please, please, please could you just remember what I am about to say right now? Just repeat over and over in your head and picture me saying to you, Believe in me, trust in me."

I decided to take him for his word and many, many times in the next few months I said those words exactly to myself to get through the difficult and lonely times.

Sometimes when I'd have a bad day and David was bothering me and things were not going well, I would cry and moan and complain and go on and on to vent and Eddie would say very clearly, "Karen! Karen! (in that adorable NY accent), Are you listening? I *love* you! I love *you*! I just love you and I will be there for you soon. Believe in me. Trust in me."

Eddie said the most romantic things to me too. He told me that he always carried a small notebook and a pen in his pocket so that when he thought of loving and romantic things that he wanted to say to me, he'd write them down so as not to forget. Such incredible thoughtfulness I'd never known.

Another day I came home from work and the package he sent me made me cry and then laugh because it made me feel so happy. It was a framed plaque that said in beautiful scroll, "And They Lived Happily Ever After." At the bottom of the plaque was written, "Karen and Eddie"

When I phoned him to let him know that I'd received his gift and how much it meant to me, he explained.

"I want you to know that your name will always come first. I'll never say Eddie and Karen; it will always be Karen and Eddie. You will always be first in my life."

Another package I received that month was another wall plaque, just as beautiful and thoughtful as the first. It read "Always kiss me goodnight" And behind the lettering, a little lighter in color were the words "Karen and Eddie."

I was able to share my happiness with Nancy and I could see that she too started to believe in Eddie more and more as he proved himself and his trustworthiness over and over again.

She'd say with a smile, "I think this man must really love you."

As I spoke to her of my upcoming trip to New York, I asked her again to keep it our secret.

I said, "If anyone wants to know where I am this time, please tell them I'm on African Safari!"

She agreed as we both laughed.

S E V E N

NEVER IN A MILLION years did I think I'd ever find myself on a romantic horse and carriage ride, sipping champagne in the middle of Central Park at Christmastime with the most incredibly kind and gentle man! But there I was; it was like a dream come true! I felt like a queen!

A couple of days earlier, as I prepared for my trip to New York, I watched the weather forecast and prayed that nothing would upset our plans. Living in the Midwest during winter can be precarious.

I'd be leaving early in the morning for New York so I got all my things packed and went to sleep for the night after talking to Eddie who calmed my nerves by telling me everything would work out just fine.

When I woke early the next morning, I looked out the window to see that it had snowed.....a substantial amount of snow, making me very nervous. I hated driving on the snowy Chicago streets, but I got in the shower and prepared myself for the day that lay ahead of me which would end up in Eddie's arms. "I can do this" I told myself. It's just a little snow.

I tip-toed out of the house so as not to awake any curious ears and when I got out to the driveway where my car was, I could see I had quite a bit of cleanup to do to try to have a visible ride to the airport. So I drew up my hood and brushed off my car, almost slipping to the ground as I did so. I laughed to myself, thinking about how odd my life had become as of late and how unusual and wonderful were the circumstances that I had found myself in often now.

It had taken courage on my part to do the things that I was doing in my life now, on my own. I was proud of myself. David had really beaten away at my self-esteem, making me believe that I couldn't stand on my own two feet and here I was doing my own thing.

Once I was on my way safely, Eddie phoned to make sure that I was okay.

I said, "The streets are pretty slippery and snowy but I can do this, I'll be okay."

"I'm going to stay on the phone with you all the way to the airport; I want to make sure that you get there safely," said Eddie.

"Even though traffic is slow, I should be fine, I've allowed plenty of extra time," I said.

"The weather is fine here in New York so as long as you get out of Chicago, you should get here without a problem, in fact you have to, I miss you so much."

"I miss you too Eddie."

I had to put the phone down a couple of times to maneuver the car safely in the snowy traffic, but it made me feel safer just knowing that he was there on the phone with me.

The sound of his voice soothed me. He made me feel like I could do anything.

If I had to, I would have walked the Sahara Desert to get to him.

I hung up with him once I arrived at the airport.

I parked my car in the long term parking area and luckily, the shuttle bus to the airport picked me up in a timely fashion from the snowy parking lot and whisked me to the proper gate area.

I breathed a sigh of relief as I stepped off the bus, realizing that I still had plenty of time before my scheduled flight. When I walked into the terminal, I was a bit shocked! There must have been three hundred people in front of me waiting to check their luggage!

I found out through listening to an airline rep up front that the computers were down and that they would be getting to each of us as soon as they possibly could. As I looked at the faces of all the people in the crowd, I tried to take comfort in the fact that I was not alone in this situation. Everyone was delayed.

I waited patiently, as well as I could anyway. The computers were up again after what seemed like hours of downtime and the line of people finally started to move, very slowly. I couldn't help but get more nervous as the time of my flight grew near. I thought if I didn't get through this line of people soon, I would surely miss it! And that just couldn't happen!

So I did what I had to do and looked at the line of people ahead of me. I started to chat with the people around me.

There was a single man in front of me who I smiled at and said, "What time is your flight?"

He said, "I've got plenty of time, it's not for a couple of hours."

"Mine is in about half an hour; would you mind terribly if I went ahead of you? I'm afraid that I might miss my flight."

He said with a smile, "Go ahead, that's fine."

A couple of other people in line were gracious enough to allow me the same kindness.

I felt such incredible relief as I finally put down my luggage onto the conveyor belt that would hopefully deliver my luggage to the right location in New York.

Of course, the gate for my flight was all the way at the opposite end of the terminal so I headed in that direction. I knew I had to still get through the security post that has become the norm for all airports now.

As I went through the security area, I realized that I had packed in my carry-on some items that were not allowed. I had always carried with me what I'd absolutely need to have, if in fact the airline ever lost my luggage. I hadn't flown in a number of years and was not as aware as I should have been.

At this point, I said to the security officer, "Please take whatever you want! I don't care! I can't miss my flight."

As I finally made my way through security, I put my shoes on, grabbed my things and moved!

Finally I was on my way to my gate, a few cosmetics short. I really didn't care. I ran to the gate, I mean I ran.............I had worked up a sweat by the time I arrived but I got there just in time! I boarded the plane and just had a moment to phone Eddie to let him know that I was on the plane and on my way to him. Oh, I was so grateful! Life was good!

He said to me, "Safe flight my darling, I'm waiting for you and can't wait to hold you."

I was so excited to see him! I put my headphones on and listened to the music on my IPod that Eddie and I had listened to together. My heart was screaming inside me with anticipation for him. I could hardly breathe thinking about being in his arms again. If I closed my eyes, I could smell him.

I realized through the sheer panic that what I was feeling was without doubt, love, and true love. I'd never felt anything like this before in my life. I never knew it existed, this feeling I was having, this longing for him.

The plane finally began to descend through the clouds and into the sunshine of a little airport on Long Island, New York. The difference in the weather here was an omen of things to come. Everything was right when I was with Eddie. Everything was good. Everything was safe.

The doors of the plane couldn't open quickly enough for me. I wanted to jump up and run in front of everyone and probably would have if I thought it would get me to him any quicker.

And so I controlled myself and I walked from the plane exit and into the luggage area of the airport where he waited for me and there he was................I breathed an incredible sigh of relief when I saw his face. The tears welled in my eyes as I ran to him and he ran to me and we embraced and we kissed. It was as if the world did not exist around us. There was no one else, just Eddie and I. I looked up into his beautiful blue eyes and that was all that I could see. There was only a blur of color around us as we held each other and could not let go. Eddie told me later that he saw an older woman looking at us and smiling as we held each other tight. I don't know how much time passed as we embraced.

By the time we approached the luggage carousel, there were only a few bags left so mine was easy to spot.

I laughed as I told Eddie, "They took some of my cosmetics at the Chicago airport; apparently the bottles were too large to carry on."

"No worries Karen, I'm just so glad that you are here safe, I can replace whatever you need."

I felt exactly that; worry free whenever I was with Eddie. I knew that he would take good care of me. I knew that I was safe with him.

All that mattered was that we were together again. We were breathing the same air and were walking on the same ground. We could hold hands again. I'd had such an incredible craving just to touch him.

He whisked up my suitcase with one hand and as he held my hand with the other, we walked out into the sunshine to his car. When we got in the car, we just looked at each other. I was so happy to be next to him it just made me laugh. It made us both laugh. We laughed until we cried. Such joy I had never felt before.

We kissed and touched, his hand just grazed my breast as he went to hug me. It sent shivers through my body, shivers of desire. He kissed me and pressed open my mouth with his tongue; his lust for me so strong and uncontrollable. His hand was on my knee and slid up my thigh as I moaned with pleasure. We burst out laughing in the midst of it all as we had begun to do as habit because of the pure joy we shared when we were together. And then he touched my face as once again, we became serious.

He cupped my face with his loving hands and looked into my eyes and said, "You are the most beautiful woman that I've ever known Karen and I love you with all my heart."

"I love you Eddie, more than words can say."

It was several minutes yet before we could control ourselves enough to be on our way.

From the airport, we drove to Port Jefferson, a beautiful little bayside town where Eddie had secured us a room in a cozy Hotel and Marina. Our room was not quite ready so we went to the restaurant that was a part of this resort for some lunch. As we scoped out the dining room, Eddie asked the host if he could seat us in the back corner that overlooked the bay and the ships and the ferries that transported people and their cars across the waters. Glass windows made up the walls around us. The view was incredibly soothing. It was a couple of weeks before Christmas and the resort was not crowded; we had the dining room all to ourselves.

As we sat down in the restaurant, Eddie helped me off with my coat and hung it on the back of my chair. As he sat down, he leaned in and kissed my neck softly and slowly. I could hear him breathe me in.

It sent shivers through me and my heart began to pound when he whispered, "You smell wonderful Karen."

"Thank you Eddie," I said.

We hardly noticed as the waitress walked up to us to get our drink order. She had that knowing look in her eyes as she smiled at us.

Eddie said, "She will have a Bloody Mary and I will have a Vodka Tonic."

"Mmmm, that sounds great," I said, "I like when you take charge like that Eddie."

I could feel his eyes upon me as he looked in the direction of my cleavage. I was wearing a black scoop neck top with a lacey blue cami underneath. His gaze spoke a thousand words of love and desire for me. There was no question that he wanted me just as much as I wanted him. It seemed like forever since we had been together.

He said, "That's the Long Island Sound right outside there. And there's the Ferry Boat. You can see the cars will drive right up onto the boat and the passengers will park their cars and walk upstairs and have a seat as they travel across to Connecticut."

I could see his mouth moving and heard vaguely what he was saying but mostly, I was noticing his dimples and his smile and his sparkling blue eyes.

I could hardly concentrate on my meal; I was dizzy with desire for him. The way that he looked at me made me feel beautiful, like never before. We had become so intimate. He devoured me with his eyes. He didn't have to say anything. We could read each other's thoughts and I knew exactly what he was thinking because I was too.

Quietly, as Eddie looked in my eyes, he said, "I want you...like I've never wanted anything before. I desire you more than I thought possible."

His word sent shivers through me.

I stroked his hand and said, "I want you too."

After a nice long lunch and a couple of drinks, we went to the front desk of the hotel to find out that our room was ready for us. We drove the car to the entrance, unloaded the luggage and breathed a sigh of relief as we got cozy in our room.

The next twenty-four hours we spent in each other's arms. Nothing else existed in that time frame; we were so lost in each other. Had there been an earthquake around us, I don't think we would have noticed. It was just Eddie and me.

He pulled the covers of the bed down as we both slipped in together. We clung to each other as if we'd never let go knowing full well that we would have to once again, at the end of our visit.

I felt shivers through my body as Eddie began to massage my arms and my back ever so gently. Our legs were intertwined like we were one. We kissed like it was the first time, so sweetly. Eddie kissed my neck and started to work his way down to my breasts. I moaned with pleasure as he touched me there.

I'd never felt such animal like lust before in my life. I wanted him so badly.

It was like we had to make up to each other the time we'd been apart....one hundred fold. And we did just that.

We made such sweet passionate love to each other. Such intimacy, I'd never known. Once we had satisfied ourselves, it was almost frightening how soon we needed each other again physically. It didn't in any way, take away from the way we had just made love. It was like, that was then and this is now and right now, we needed each other again. Such a physical need, I'd never experienced before.

Loving someone, the way that I loved Eddie, made the act of making love a whole different thing than anything I'd ever known before.

It had been five months now since I'd met Eddie on line. There was no doubt in my mind that he was the one. I could feel in my heart that he was the love of my life. It was funny to me to think that it took me more than half my life to find him, to find true love. Certainty like I felt surely must only come once in a lifetime to some of us, those of us who are lucky enough to feel. I'm sure that there are others who will never find what I had found with Eddie.

E I G H T

W E WOKE UP EARLY the next day. It was always so joyful to wake next to him. This morning as I opened my eyes, Eddie was right there smiling at me.

He said, "We are going to Manhattan today to see the sights. I have our whole day planned, let's get ready to go!"

"So really, who am I to argue?" I said as I laughed. We had bubbly conversation and drank coffee as we prepared ourselves for the day ahead. Eddie loved doing things for me. He wanted to make my coffee and help me to straighten up the room before we left. I couldn't help but see just how different he was from David. I'd never been treated so well before in my life and I was really starting to trust it and to enjoy it.

I thanked him for every kindness he'd shown me until he said, "You don' have to thank me for everything that I do for you. I do these things because I love you."

I couldn't help myself though. I was just not used to such thoughtfulness.

He said, "I want to make up to you all the crap that you've tolerated in your life; all the unkindness."

It seemed silly to me that he would want to make up to me all the wrongs that someone else had put me through. I thought it was one of the kindest things that anyone had ever said to me and he reminded me often. He started to make promises to me about our future.

They were promises of a good and calm and happy life together, which were things I hadn't had in my life for a very long time.

He'd say, "If you agree to plan a future with me, your life will be sweet. All you have to do is get up and breathe. I'll do all the rest. I love you and want to take care of you."

I was only a bit skeptical because I'd previously thought that all men were alike. I know now that that is certainly not the case, not the case at all. I wanted to believe Eddie and I hoped in my heart that it would just be a matter of time till I could trust him totally.

It was a cold but sunny day so we bundled up and headed out of the hotel and into Eddie's car. Our plan was to take the train from Ronkonkoma to Manhattan. It had been awhile since Eddie had taken the train so we drove around trying to find the station where we could board. As we looked, I could see that he was getting just a bit frustrated because he wanted the day to go perfectly. Again David's behavior popped into my head. It was so off the wall, that had it been David in the same situation, he would have been cussing and swearing at me and he would have driven home as he blamed me for everything once again going wrong and cancelled our plans. After having lived with and tolerated David for as many years as I did, it was hard for this thought not to enter into my head.

As I sat next to Eddie in the car, I looked over and waited. I was waiting for him to blow up like David used to. I was waiting for him to start yelling. I almost ducked in anticipation.

I was just so delightfully surprised when there was not even a sign of irritation. In fact, once we found the train station finally, we realized that we had missed the train we wanted and would have to wait an hour or so to catch the next one.

And so this is what Eddie said to me next. "Well, I've really screwed up, I can't believe I couldn't find the train station! So there's only one thing that I can do to make it up to you! Let's go, we're going jewelry shopping!"

And with that we were off to the local jewelry department, laughing our heads off! We found a beautiful necklace, the second one that

Eddie bought for me that had a butterfly pendant on it but it was gorgeous and I couldn't resist! The butterfly continued to be for us a symbol of our long distance love and wanting to be together no matter what mode of transportation it would take to make that happen.

It struck me that we took several modes of transportation in that one day. We drove back to the station and got on the train and headed towards Manhattan. Here I was with this big strong man next to me, this former cop; I was so in love with him! I was beaming, so proud to be with him! He was so protective of me, he made sure that I sat by the window out of the way of the bustling crowds of people that came down the aisle past us. We held hands all the way there and kissed each other and laughed and just reveled in each other's company. People around us probably thought we were intoxicated or just plain crazy the way that we laughed. It was such a wonderful crazy! It was so healing to be with Eddie.

We got off the train when it stopped in the underground subway station. We walked through and up the stairs into the sunshine of the day and downtown Manhattan. I'd been familiar with the hustle and bustle of a big city because I was from the Chicago area but was still struck by the enormity of the city and the crowds of people all over. So Eddie held me close to him as we waited in line for a cab, our next mode of transportation of the day.

As we got into the cab, Eddie said to the driver, "Take us to the Plaza!"

The Plaza Hotel was to be our first stop in Manhattan.

As we stepped out of the cab in front of the hotel, Eddie led me in the direction of the front stairs where a tall man in a highly decorated uniform stood guard and opened the door for us. I could almost imagine the celebrities that had been here before us.

As we walked into the main lobby we could see that it was quite majestic this Christmastime with an enormous and beautifully decorated tree next to the staircase that led up to a balcony of sorts. It was the kind of staircase where you might have imagined seeing Vivien Leigh walking down in her huge gown to the open arms of Clark Gable in "Gone with the Wind."

The room was bustling with people coming and going. There was an open bar right in the lobby where we got some Martinis to sip on.

Eddie chose a table off to the side so that we'd get a full view of whatever might be happening. We laughed as we sat down and just drank in the atmosphere and pretended that we belonged there.

There was of course, Christmas music being played on a Grand Piano by a talented musician and the mood of the whole place was that of a joyous occasion. We laughed and kissed and whispered to each other. Anyone looking at us must have guessed that we were on our honeymoon; we were so immersed in our love together.

I didn't know what Eddie had planned next; he only said, "We are just going to kick back and relax here awhile until it starts to get dark out and then I'll tell you what the next surprise is!"

"I am just so happy to be here with you Eddie, I love you." I said.

"And I love you baby."

As dusk began to fall and as we finished sipping on our second martini, Eddie said, "Okay, it's time to get moving Karen, let's go across the street."

So we bundled up in our coats and scarves and headed to the front doors of the hotel. We walked outside and as we looked across the busy street in front of the Plaza, I saw there were several Horse Drawn Carriages with Drivers waiting for their passengers.

Eddie said, "Take your pick, choose your carriage my lady and we'll be off."

I laughed out loud; he made me feel so happy!

As we boarded a maroon covered carriage with flowers draped across the sides, I looked around at the scenery around us. It was like a moment out of a Norman Rockwell Painting, so serene. Central Park was the backdrop for the waiting Carriages; the snow covered paths looked beautiful under the moonlight.

The carriage was pulled by a large black horse; it was cold enough that you could see his breath as he snorted and moved his huge mane up and down as if to welcome us. The Driver, with his Top Hat and Regal Coat, helped drape us in the warm blanket he had stored up front in a cubby of sorts where he kept his supplies from falling off the mostly open carriage.

So Eddie and I had no choice, of course, but to cuddle up under the blanket as we took off for our ride through Central Park. It was all a part of Eddie's plan to woo me, to knock me off of my feet. He was doing such a good job of it!

The ride was beautiful through the park. We passed just a few other carriages as we rode to the middle of the park. I was feeling so happy that my face began to strain from smiling so big for so long. Can you imagine feeling that happy? I could have never imagined that myself, because I'd never before felt the euphoria that I was feeling now.

I could feel Eddie looking at me as I reveled in the ride and took it all in.

He held me closer and whispered in my ear, " Karen, I want you to be just this happy for the rest of your life. I hope you will allow me to do that for you."

"I'm loving all of this Eddie, it's just as wonderful as you promised, and I love being here with you. I love being anywhere with you."

And then in the middle of Central Park, Eddie pulled two small glasses from his pocket and a small bottle of champagne and poured us both a glass. I could not have envisioned anything so romantic before. I thought my heart might explode right out of my chest because of the love I was feeling for this man.

As we toasted, Eddie said to me, "Karen, I love you with all my heart and all I want is for us to be together forever, you are my life."

I felt so warm inside even with the chill of the night air all around us. It felt so right to be with him; it felt like I could breathe a huge sigh of relief. I felt like I was exactly where I should be............with Eddie.

"And I love you too Eddie," I said.

We sipped on our drinks and kissed and whispered to each other and laughed as we drove through the park. Surely, I thought this must be what it feels like to be in heaven.

Our ride came to an end at a beautiful spot, right near a very famous restaurant called, "Tavern on the Green." There must have been a million lights all around the outside and also on the inside. You could see right through the windows that took up the full length in some parts of the walls. We stopped to take some pictures of each other in front of the place. I was so glad that I had brought my camera to try to capture the magic of the evening. I knew that once I went back home, I'd only have the photos and the memories of this day to sustain me until Eddie and I were together once again.

We walked a bit as I anticipated what Eddie might have in store for us next. We could see our breath as we spoke and walked; we were both so excited. I couldn't help but notice what good physical shape that he was in for a man ten years my senior; you would never have known it. We walked at a quick pace and never once was he out of breath; I realized then that having been a cop and walking the beats that he did, had left him very healthy and strong. It was important to me that a man I might be with, be health conscious because David had been so neglectful of his well being. It was very hard to watch someone purposely hurting themselves that way.

Eddie held my hand so securely; I loved how tall he was next to me. Our next destination he told me, was more than walking distance. So when we were not able to hail a cab because of the crowds of people in Manhattan this night, Eddie actually got the attention of a driver who was pulling a small cart enclosed in what looked like plastic windows on its sides. He was pulling the cart by bicycle. It seemed funny but there were several of them around so we got on. I laughed out loud as I saw cars and cabs wiz right past us at speeds much greater than we traveled. When I think back on it; it makes me laugh still because I doubt that it was the safest way to go but it got us from point A to point B and you had to admire the way the driver pedaled his little heart out to get us to our destination.

As we came upon it, you could not escape the enormity of the Rockefeller Center Christmas Tree. The driver wished us well as Eddie tipped him for the ride and we disembarked to get closer to the tree.

There were crowds of people around us I'm sure, but I hardly noticed. Eddie was aware that I'm a bit leery around big groups of people but being here with him, I didn't give it a second thought. He walked in front of me through the crowd as if to shield me from harm. It was just so comfortable and safe being with him.

The enormity of the tree was overwhelming; it brought tears to my eyes to be here. It was magnificent! Eddie watched my excited reaction.

"I'm so happy to be the one to introduce you to something so moving as this. It makes me feel so good to give this to you."

"It's breathtaking," I said.

It was an incredible moment to be able to share together.

I'd seen the tree before on the television news but there was certainly nothing quite like being there right in front of it. It was quite the sight to behold! It was bigger than I'd even imagined and so beautiful. Millions of lights surrounded the tree branches. It was topped with a huge colorful star and you couldn't help but notice the nightscape of tall city buildings and lights all around it.

The Zamboni smoothed the surface as the ice skaters glided by on the rink in front of the tree. The moment was again surreal, like so many I had experienced with this sweet man whom I was feeling more and more of a bond with.

I snapped several photos and then Eddie asked a passerby to take a picture of the two of us together with the tree in the background.

We began to grow cold as we realized that it was probably about time to head back to the Inn where we were staying. Eddie wrapped his arm around me and I held him around the waist as we made our way back to the train station which was now walking distance from where we were.

Before we knew it, we were back on the train to Ronkonkoma. The train ride back was so calm; I leaned my head onto Eddie's shoulder as the train raced back to Long Island and thought about the day's events. It had been magical. As we got back into his car on Long Island, it started to snow lightly. It was such a beautiful night; the perfect ending to a perfect day.

We were happy to get back to our warm and cozy room at the Inn. We drank hot chocolates and recounted the day's events. Nothing could spoil the day that we'd had.

As Eddie began to kiss me though, I couldn't help but dread the fact that we would have to say goodbye again by the end of the next day. Friday was the day that I was scheduled to go home; my brother was hosting the annual family Christmas party on Saturday and I needed to be there. My kids and my parents and my brothers and sisters were expecting to see me there. The party had been highly anticipated every year. It would be very unusual if all family members were not there. Except for Nancy, no one else knew where I was. I had to make my appearance at the party and I actually thought that the party would distract me once I had gotten home and perhaps I'd be able to, for just a moment, think about something besides Eddie.

I knew that the same thought was in Eddie's head too. We could both tell what was on the other's mind just by looking into each other's eyes. There was no need to say it out loud. In fact, saying it out loud would have made us sadder so we tried to ignore that fact the best that we could.

When we got back to our room, I took off my shoes and started to get comfortable. Eddie came up from behind me and I could feel his breath on my neck as he kissed my shoulders. I tilted my head to the side and sighed, drinking in his touch, as he kissed the back of my head. As his lips wandered, he unbuttoned my blouse from behind me and let it fall to the floor. It sent shivers through my body as I looked forward to the passion that would follow. I turned to face him.

He kissed my lips and carried me to the bed then and we became lost in each other once again. We made love desperately, always desperately, almost like we may never have the chance again. It was as if the more passionate we were, the longer it may last before we would become, once again, so wanton for each other.

We made love that night for hours before we fell asleep, exhausted into each other's arms.

N I N E

THE NEXT MORNING WE woke early. I'm still trying to understand the kind of love that I felt for Eddie, never having felt this kind of intensity before, because the moment that I opened my eyes, I needed him again, physically.

After we made love, I prepared myself for the day; taking a shower and fixing my hair while Eddie made coffee. When I came out of the bathroom, there was a wrapped Christmas gift waiting for me on the bed. Eddie smiled at me as I dug into my suitcase for the gift I had brought for him.

He said, "Go ahead, you go first."

"All right," I said.

I was so excited that I was laughing with anticipation and was so surprised when I first opened his card and discovered that I had bought him the exact same greeting card! I couldn't believe it! We lived in different states, had done our shopping in different states and had managed to purchase the same Christmas card for each other. So when I realized this, I insisted that he open his card even before I opened my gift.

We looked at each other with disbelief as we read the card entitled, "For the One I Love" The inside of the card read, "Before you came along, I'm sure snow sparkled just as brightly, carols rang out just as sweetly, and Christmas lights twinkled as merrily as they do now. But ever since we fell in love, it feels as if the holidays were invented just for us to share, and the only gift I ever really wanted has been given to me….. the gift of you."

We both teared up at the sweet sentiment.

To us, it was just another indication of how right this whole thing between us was.

I opened my gift then and was thrilled to see that Eddie had bought me a laptop computer, complete with a leather carrying case.

"Oh my gosh Eddie! I love it, this is wonderful, thank you."

"I'm so happy to be able to get that for you. Having your own now will allow us more time to chat and to play Scrabble," said Eddie.

Eddie opened his gift then to see that I had bought him a collection of movies with one of his favorite actors playing the lead role. He loved it. I enclosed a note saying that this would be the first of "Our" collection of movies to watch together.

We decided to go to the restaurant at the resort where we stayed once more and to sit by the windows looking out on the bay and have some breakfast. We drank Mimosas with our meal as we noticed that the snow was coming down a little harder now.

We talked about what a wonderful time we'd had together these past couple of days and when Eddie might fly out to me again. Eddie explained to me that as soon as he was able to clear up some matters here on Long Island that if I allowed, he wanted to move to my hometown permanently. Oh, how I wanted to believe him! ………but I wasn't convinced even yet of his commitment. I'd been disappointed so often in my life. His whole family was here on Long Island, he had lived here all his life. Would he really move all those miles to be with me? I tried to wrap my mind around the whole idea.

And then he looked into my eyes and kissed me and I almost believed that anything could happen. All we could see was each other.

Before we were to head to the airport, Eddie said, "Let's go shopping once more, I'd like to get a few things for you. Let me get you whatever you need, I want to take care of you."

So we went to the store and as we did, we noticed that the streets were starting to get a little slippery with the snow. While we were in the store, there was some fun music playing and being in the giddy mood that I was whenever I was with Eddie, I started dancing down the aisles just a bit and as I did, I noticed that he was doing the same moves as me which made me laugh so hard that I began to cry.

I had always thought that in life, laughter is absolutely the best medicine there is and it felt so good to just let loose and go with the moment. I'm sure that people around us noticed but we didn't care, we were just so lost in each other. We were just so full of joy when we were together!

We headed back to the Inn, knowing that we'd have to pack up our things soon and head to the airport. As we drove to the Inn, the snow seemed to be coming down even harder. There were a couple of roads we traveled that were on an incline and the cars around us were having a bit of trouble maneuvering on them because of the snow.

We got back to our room and once more made love desperately, knowing that it would be several weeks until we could be together again. We held each other so tight, as if the closer we held each other, the longer the hours before we would long for each other again. But that effort was futile because the longing was always there for him. Always………..

We were both silent afterwards as we cleaned up our room, lost in our own thoughts, feeling too emotional to speak.

As we walked out of the hotel, I looked back at the Inn, wanting to etch in my mind forever the sight of it.

We got back into the car and headed in the direction of the airport.

It was at this point that I said to Eddie, "I wonder if there will be any delays at the airport because of the weather."

Eddie said, "Maybe you should call the airline to see if there are any issues that are weather related."

When I called, the automated answering service told me that my flight would take off according to schedule.

We had a little time to spare and Eddie and I were hungry. It had been hours since we'd had breakfast. He wanted to take me to a genuine NY Deli so that's where we headed. Eddie reveled in showing me things that were signature to his part of New York.

I laughed when he spoke to the woman behind the counter. I was so struck by the accent I heard as they spoke. When Eddie was in his native New York, his accent seemed even more exaggerated.

The sandwiches that she had made for us were huge and they looked delicious.

When we got back into the car, the weather had gotten even messier.

Eddie suggested, "Maybe you had better call the airline again, this weather is looking messier by the minute."

"Okay," I said.

I put the phone on Speaker so that Eddie could hear it too.

We both heard it at the same time.

The message said, "All flights in and out of the airport are cancelled until further notice."

My mouth dropped open, "Oh my gosh, I can't go home today."

And then we were both laughing.

"We get to spend one more night together," I said.

"Yes, we do!" Eddie said.

I was so excited one moment and then aghast the next! All of a sudden it dawned on me! I thought of my family back home and the Christmas party that would take place without me tomorrow and how in the world I was going to explain to everyone where I was!

"What will I tell my kids? What about the party tomorrow?" I gasped!

Eddie said, "Just take a breath Karen, we will handle it."

My mind was racing, trying to figure out what to do.

How would I explain this to them? They were expecting to see me at the Christmas party. I was waiting for the right time to tell them about my relationship with Eddie and why I had kept it to myself for so long.

I realized that I had to tell them the truth and now was as good a time as any. I had no choice. Don't they say that everything happens for a reason? Just the way it's supposed to?

Eddie and I drove very cautiously and slowly to a hotel that was close to the airport. When we got inside the lobby, I told Eddie that I had to call my kids right away. I was nervous about it and wanted to just get it done. I knew that they might be angry with me. They might wonder if I'd lost my mind. But I knew that mostly they would be concerned for my safety.

Eddie showed me again in that moment, what a kind and respectful man he was and left me alone to make my calls.

I phoned each of my three children and just came out with the truth.

I told them that I was in NY with a man I'd met a few months before. I let them know that I could not be at the Christmas party as expected.

It's amazing to me, to this day, how different all my children are.

My oldest daughter started to cry when I told her.

"Are you crazy?" she yelled at me. "How could you do this? How do you know this man? Aren't you still married?"

"I understand how insane all this sounds to you. I never would have expected this from myself. I'm sorry that you are upset. I'm just letting you know where I am right now and that I will not be at the Christmas party tomorrow."

"What am I supposed to tell everyone?" she said through her tears.

"How can I go if you won't be there? I don't even want to go," she said.

She was clearly shocked and I couldn't blame her.

I told her, "Please just tell them that I called you and that I took an unexpected trip and am stuck out of town because of bad weather."

Of course I knew in my heart how difficult this would be for all my family to swallow because up until this point in time, I had been totally predictable.

I said, "I'm so sorry to have put you in this situation. We will talk about this more when I get home. You can ask me whatever you want and I will explain it to you the best that I can. I love you."

As she hung up the phone, I knew that what she was feeling most surely was fear for my safety.

When I spoke to my son, he was a bit more laid back about what I had to tell him. I think that he had known for a while that something was up with me. I'd not been behaving quite the same as always. My kids were so much more perceptive than David had ever been. They knew me well.

He said, "I love you Mom but are you nuts? Please get home safely and we will talk about this."

My youngest daughter took the news the best. Being that she was my baby, we had an almost ESP like sense about each other. We could often tell what the other was thinking without saying a word. She was the most touched in a guttural sort of way by all the bad things that had gone on between David and I, and she longed for my happiness and well being as well as her own. She was fiercely protective of me.

I could almost hear the relief in her voice as she said, "Mom, I've known that something's been different about you lately. I need to know everything about this man that you are with. Are you sure that you are okay?"

"Yes," I said, "I'm sure. I feel safer than I have in a long time."

She said, "I will miss you so much at the party. Please be careful and get back home to us. I love you."

"I love you too. I'll call you as soon as I get back."

It was a shock to all of them, to say the least. I'd always been so level headed.

They always knew what to expect from me but this situation had thrown them all a curve ball for sure.

I realized in that moment too, how special and wonderful it had been to keep all of the details of this relationship with Eddie a secret up until this point. It was the first time in my life that I was thinking of myself first.

But I also knew that telling my family would be the beginning of a New Chapter to our Love Affair.

I had told myself through the secrecy of it all, that no matter how this thing ended up, I would be that much smarter and a better person for having known Eddie.

They knew. I realized that I would have to deal with each of my children when I returned home. It was a relief in some ways to have it over with.

Eddie and I were lucky then to find this hotel had an available room. We checked in and got cozy, not really knowing whether or not, I'd be able to fly home the next day. It all depended on the unpredictable weather.

We reveled in the bonus of being together one more night than we had expected. That was the first time, I think, that I felt like this fairy tale relationship might actually become a reality.

We watched one of the movies that I had bought him for Christmas and relished the sandwiches we had purchased from the deli. It was one of those nights that you just wanted to cozy up and stay inside where it was warm; where you felt protected. It almost felt like we could have been a married couple who had been together for a long time; we were so comfortable together. My best friend, Eddie and I.

I felt so protected by him. He was my Knight in Shining Armor.

As we sat on the couch, my feet were in his lap.

He said, "Would you mind if I massage your feet?"

"I would love that," I said.

As he touched my feet, I felt so relaxed. He had such a gentle touch and massaged so lovingly. He picked them up one at a time and kissed every toe so gently. And then his loving hands slid up my legs until he reached the tie on my robe and as he opened it, he travelled up my body and kissed me slowly all the way to my breasts.

My body shuddered in anticipation.

He carried me to the bed then and we made love like it was the first time; it was always like the first time, only better. The more often we made love, the more he was getting to know exactly what moved me most.

This evening felt like such a bonus to us both.

We melted into each other. I felt like together, we were one.

We couldn't even talk about the next day's departure; it was too emotional.

We fell asleep in each other's arms and slept soundly, just as it should have been.

It was obvious the next morning, because the weather had cleared, that I would in fact be going home.

I phoned the airport to find that my flight had been rescheduled for that afternoon. We had a long breakfast in the downstairs restaurant and drank coffee together. We talked and laughed, and languished in being side by side.

It was time to head to the airport so we loaded up the car and were on our way. We were both lost in our own thoughts as we headed to the airport. We always dreaded this part of our visit.

I checked in my luggage with the Sky cab, all I had left to do was get through security and be on my way. The airport on Long Island is small in comparison to Chicago and going through security would only take a minute. We could see that there was nobody waiting so we chose to stay together every last minute possible. We sat close together, Eddie's arm around me. We sat just a few hundred feet from the escalator that would take me up to the entrance for my flight. We could hardly speak; our hearts were breaking at the thought of once again, being one thousands mile apart.

Eddie said, "I can't stand that you are leaving. I feel so helpless. I want to go with you. I want to protect you and keep you safe. I want to make your life easier. So when you have to go up that escalator, I'm begging you..........please don't look back. I can't stand the thought. Please don't look back."

So when I knew that I couldn't wait any longer for fear I'd miss my flight, I got up and without a word, I hugged and kissed him one more time as my eyes welled up with tears and I walked away.

And as I had promised, I didn't look back as I went up the escalator. I could feel his eyes behind me but I didn't look back as I wiped the tears from my face. I knew if I looked back, I would run right back to him.

I was on my own again and I knew I had no choice but to go home. I went to the assigned gate and stood in line to board my flight. My phone rang as I stood in line and it was him. I didn't care, didn't even notice that as we spoke, my tears were running down my face. I'm sure that the people around me wondered why I cried but it didn't matter. Nothing else mattered at that moment...nothing.

He said, "I love you more than you will ever know. If there were a word that means more than love, I would use it."

I could barely get the words out but I said, "I feel the same way."

Eddie said, "I promise you that it will not be much longer before we can be together all the time. Have a safe flight and please call me when you land."

"I will," I said.

"Karen...Karen...can you hear me? I love you...I love you," he said as I could hear him choking up with tears himself.

He told me later that he couldn't move for a while, just sat there in his seat in the airport lobby. He felt so depressed and helpless. When he finally got up, he went to his car and drove to the end of the runway and parked in a little bank parking lot that was right outside the airport and being that McArthur Airport is so small and has so few flights, he knew without question when the plane that I was on was moving down the runway preparing for takeoff.

He told me later, "I waved to the plane as you took off and I cried, I just felt so helpless."

The flight home was just a blur for me but became reality once again upon landing back in Chicago. As I waited for my luggage at the carousel, I spoke to Eddie on the phone to ensure him that I'd landed safely. I told him I'd call him again once I was safe in my car.

The weather was cold and dreary as I dragged my suitcase from the shuttle bus to my car in the mostly deserted long term parking lot. The snow around my car was deep! I shivered in the cold when I tried the lock on the car door only to realize that it was frozen and covered in ice. Now too I noticed that all the windows were full of frozen snow and thick ice as well. I just wanted to cry, I'd forgotten my gloves and all I wanted was to be warm and safe in Eddie's arms again.

But I smiled as I remembered that Eddie had prepared me before I'd left him and I went into my suitcase to find the snow equipment he'd insisted on purchasing for me, just in case.

There was a spray that thawed the lock on the car door.

As I was finally able to get inside, I said out loud, "Thank you Eddie."

I started the car up and threw my suitcase into the back seat. I then got to the business of cleaning up the outside so that I could see out the windows. I was very anxious to be on my way.

There I was, standing in foot high snow with no boots on as I reached into my suitcase and pulled out another De-Icing Spray that Eddie insisted I have for the windshield. It worked like a charm, much to my relief.

I sat in the car then, turned the heat on full blast, and let the rest of the ice melt all the while thinking how much I already missed Eddie. It was physically painful for me. As my eyes welled with tears, I told myself, "Get it together girl, you're on your own now, let's get home."

As I pulled out of the Airport parking lot, I dialed Eddie's number and put him on speaker phone so that I could talk to him all the way home. He always made me feel safe and loved…always loved.

Eddie was feeling lonely and depressed already as well.

He said, "I can't stand the thought of going back home to my dungeon with Margaret. It's so depressing there, I miss you so much."

"I know Eddie, I feel the same way as you," I said.

"I just want to be with you always." Eddie said.

"Me too."

"I'm at the bar having a drink, reliving every moment we had together. It's the only way I can get through the time we have to wait to be together again," he said.

"I know….I know, I love you Eddie."

As soon as I pulled up in front of my sister's place, Eddie said, "Go inside, take a hot shower and get warm."

"Okay," I said, "I'll talk to you later handsome."

It was not until then that I noticed that my pants were soaking wet and cold from the knees down. I felt warm inside though, as I realized that Eddie was taking better care of me from one thousand miles away, better than David ever did right next to me. It was almost like Eddie was right next to me here, hugging me and protecting me, keeping me safe and warm.

I was glad when I got inside the house, there was no one home. They were still at the Christmas Party that I had missed so I was able to go upstairs to my room lost in my thoughts.

After I took a hot shower and as I started to unpack my bags, my sister and her family came home. One of my out-of-town sisters was with them.

We are a close family and word spreads fast! Both my sisters came upstairs anxious to know everything about my trip.

I gushed with some of the romantic details. I smiled and laughed as they ooohed and ahhhed when they heard of the carriage ride in Central Park and drinks at the Plaza and seeing the tree in Rockefeller Center. It was fun and it helped to lessen the pain just a bit of how much I missed him.

When I was alone again, I crawled into bed; I was exhausted from the trip. And like every night now, I spoke to Eddie as I got cozy under the electric blanket that he had sent me to keep me warm. It wasn't long before I was fast asleep, dreaming of him and all the possibilities that lay ahead for us.

T E N

B EFORE I KNEW IT, the alarm was going off and it was time to head off to work. It was just a few days before Christmas now and I was in the process of deciding how this holiday would go and what plans I would make with my kids. I knew there would be lots of discussion about my relationship with Eddie, lots of questions to answer. I was ready.

I'd always had a close bond with my children. I didn't see that changing now either. I suspected they might be aggravated with me for not telling them sooner but I knew that after we spoke they would be good. We'd been through a lot of things together, especially this last year with my divorce and we always came out fine at the end. That is because of the love and trust we have in each other.

My work week came to an end. Every day all day long, I thought about Eddie. And Eddie thought about me. We talked on the phone several times a day, we texted each other constantly and we played Scrabble on line. We instant messaged each other on the laptop computer that he gave me for Christmas.

Every night would end up the same. I would crawl into bed under my warm blanket and talk softly to him until I couldn't keep my eyes open any longer. And every morning, he was my first thought.

As we talked about Eddie's next trip to see me in January, we both wondered how we would survive the holidays without being able to touch each other, without being able to kiss, without being able to share the same space and breath. But we knew we had no choice for now and we'd have to make the best of things.

Sometimes I'd get to feeling really down and he could hear it in my voice in an instant and he'd do whatever he could to be as supportive as he could be from where he was.

I sometimes felt doubtful and my tears would give me away to Eddie. There was still a bit of uncertainty in me that things might not end up the way we had hoped.

Eddie would remind me, "Whenever you feel unsure or afraid, just remember these words, Believe in me, Trust in me."

Everything that he had promised me so far had in fact, happened. So in reality I had no reason to doubt him. Those words had become my mantra. I would say them to myself, and sometimes out loud. That phrase helped me to get through those days.

It was Christmas Eve and I had planned on going over to my daughter's apartment. Both my daughters lived together since my split with David. I had always hosted Christmas day dinner for my children and my grandson so this holiday was a big change and adjustment for all of us. The plan was that I'd stay with my daughters for a couple of days and that we'd get through the holidays together.

So I drove over to their place, I remember the weather was really bad, traffic was very slow. The snow was coming down heavy; there were deep ruts in the street where your tires had no choice but to go.

On my way, I spoke to Eddie on the phone.

I cried, "How will I get through these days without you?"

Eddie said, "You are strong Karen, stronger than me, you will get through this time; we both will, somehow."

"My body aches for you."

"I know how you feel, the physical pain is huge. I can't eat and I can't sleep but somehow I will get through this charade with Margaret and my family here. I can hardly wait to tell her I want a divorce. I want to shout from the rooftops that I'm in love with you," he said.

"Can I text you whenever I can't bear it?"

"Yes, of course, my phone will always be in my pocket," Eddie said.

I actually looked forward to the conversations that I knew would take place with my daughters, explaining my relationship with Eddie. I looked forward to the questions and to the opportunity, finally, to tell them all about him.

Eddie had his hands full too because for the last time, he had to pretend that everything was okay between Margaret and him. His children were coming over for Christmas dinner and he wanted to spend one more holiday, all of them together. He had promised me that after the holidays, he would break the news to Margaret, that he wanted a divorce. All I kept thinking through these times were his words, "Believe in me, Trust in me."

Christmas actually turned out quite nice after all. I so enjoy my daughters' company. We had "THE" conversation and there were lots of questions as I knew there would be and there were also tears, as we talked it all out.

My younger daughter said, "Mom, how could you have been so reckless to have met this man that you hardly knew?"

I said, "If I were to ever find out that you had done the same thing, I'd want to strangle you for taking such a risk! So I understand what you are saying."

She said, "Why didn't you tell me that you were going to New York? What if something had happened to you?"

I explained, "I know that this is totally unlike me, but after speaking to Eddie for about six weeks at great length, I felt a compulsion like I've never experienced before to meet him. It was almost like a power outside of myself was pushing me uncontrollably in his direction."

My older daughter was engaged to be married at that time and when I explained to her the similarities between Eddie and her own fiancé, she softened.

I said, "Eddie is the kindest and gentlest man that I've ever met. He is a gentle giant of sorts just like your Patrick."

She said through her tears, "Okay, how could I not like him if he's anything like my Pat."

"All that I can tell you both is that I've never felt this kind of love before and I've never felt happier."

Both my daughters could see how my face lit up when I spoke of Eddie, anybody back then would have known how sincerely I felt for him just by looking at me, as I spoke of him.

So we ate our Christmas dinner that day and we giggled as moms and daughters do, as we ate dessert before dinner. We laughed as we talked about how different this holiday was from any we had experienced before. We talked about how much smarter all of us were becoming and how much stronger because of all the things that had changed in this past year. We just thoroughly enjoyed each other's company, more so than we had in a long time. In the past with David, things had become so uncomfortable for all of us, not knowing when he might blow up, or say something stupid, or spoil our family get-togethers.

So we all got through Christmas that year. I got through it with my children's support and Eddie got through his in New York.

I spent New Year's Eve that year at my sister's house. All my kids were there and so was my grandson. It helped so much to be with people that I loved so that I could bear to be away from Eddie. He was alone in Long Island, all alone.

I was so sad for him when the New Year rang in there in New York. He spent that moment all alone in front of his TV, like he had many years previously.

I said to him, "Tell me please that this will be the last holiday that we will spend apart."

"That's the only way that I can bear this loneliness today," Eddie said.

"It will definitely be a happier year coming up my love," I said.

"Happy New Year Karen, I love you with all my heart and want to be with you always."

"Happy New Year Eddie, I can't wait to be with you again."

When I went to bed that night, Eddie and I spoke again, he under his covers and me under mine. He slept in a bedroom in the basement he again referred to as his dungeon.

The only thing that got us through those days was making our plans for our next visit. We spent all our days and nights talking about when we would be together again. And when we weren't able to speak, we were thinking about our next time together.

Once again, the countdown began. As I waited for him, my days were lonely, people around me but lonely, so lonely for him. I had never felt such a yearning for anything else ever in my life.

I came home from work one day to a package at the door for me. Eddie had previously asked me to email him the pictures I had taken while in NY with him. In the package was a coffee mug and a travel thermos for coffee; both of them emblazoned with all the pictures I had sent him from our last visit.

There were pictures of us in the horse drawn carriage and pictures of us in front of the Rockefeller Center.

It made me cry, of course. It was just so sweet of him; he had them specially made for me.

He was always sending me things. It got so my sister's kids would just put the packages outside my bedroom door and wait for me to show them what he had sent me.

They would say, "Wow, Aunt Karen, this man must really love you," and I would just smile knowing I couldn't possibly put into words the way we felt about each other.

But I did tell my nieces, over and over again, that every woman deserves to be treated like Eddie was treating me. That fact was finally sinking into my head. I deserved to be treated with respect and kindness always.

My grandson was six years old at the time; he and I had a very special bond.

He was my first and only grandchild. Ian was born in a rural town, about an hour and a half outside of Chicago.

The night that he was born was magical; we were all there. I stood right outside the room where he was born and walked down the hospital hallway with my son as he carried him to the Nursery for his first bath. It was such a small hospital that Ian was the only baby there in the maternity department.

My son and Ian's mom lived with us in our home for the first year of his life. I have found that kids are so accepting of any situation around them if you are just open and honest with them.

After I'd left David, I had explained to Ian.

"Grandma and Grandpa are not going to be living together anymore."

"Why not?" Ian asked.

I said, "Sometimes people are just not meant to live together anymore and Grandpa and I will be happier this way."

He looked rather sad but I explained further.

"It won't make any difference to you though. Grandpa and I will always love you no matter what, that will never change. You will just see us separately now, that's all."

I realized that now was a good time to tell him about Eddie too, knowing in my heart now that Eddie was going to be a permanent person in my life and in turn Ian's life as well.

I told him, "There is a new man in my life who you will be meeting soon Ian. His name is Eddie and I think that you will love him. He is a very kind man and he treats Grandma like a queen."

I could see from the smile on his face that he was pleased. Kids are so smart. Ian had very often seen the turmoil and un- kindnesses that had gone on between David and me.

I laughed when I later found out that when Ian was with David, he proclaimed "Eddie treats grandma like a queen."

Maybe it gave David some food for thought!

I can hardly explain the euphoria that I felt every time I picked Eddie up from the airport. I looked so forward to the whole ritual of preparing for him. I would decide what to wear upon his arrival days in advance. I would make sure that my hair was perfect. I'd go get a pedicure which is one of my favorite luxuries. My bag would be packed and ready to go the night before.

I'll never forget how he would look standing there at the end of the drive at the airport just beaming with enthusiasm as I pulled up. He was so tall and handsome; his sparkling blue eyes matched the blue jacket that he wore that winter. I loved to look over at him as he drove and just drink him in.

I remember that January visit was one of the coldest in Chicago history. It was the kind of cold that hurts and all you want to do is just stay inside and stay warm.

I was so happy that he arrived safely with no weather delays. Once I picked him up, it would have been fine with me if we just stayed in our room. It was like heaven to be with him. That's exactly what we did; we hardly went out for anything.

I find cooking to be totally therapeutic and I've been told that I'm very good at it so I decided to surprise Eddie with a couple of my dishes. He was very surprised and very impressed.

We spent our days making love and talking and watching movies and indulging in our favorite foods.

Every time we made love, it was more passionate and more satisfying than the time before, as if each time we knew each other's everything better.

Eddie had broken the news to Margaret of his decision to divorce her. It was difficult for both of them, he being the kind man that he is not wanting to hurt anyone, but also knowing that it was time to be happy in his life and to move forward.

We talked now of serious plans. Eddie was trying to figure out how long it would take for him to take care of all the business that would be involved. He had lived in NY for all his life. His whole family was there. I guess there were still some parts of me, even then that still doubted that he would actually do this for me, to leave everything behind.

Every time I felt this doubt, Eddie would remind me of his promise, "Trust in me, believe in me." I hung on to those words; I had no other choice really.

E L E V E N

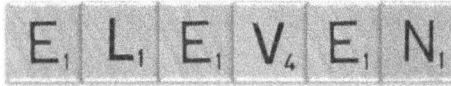

WHEN EDDIE RETURNED TO Long Island in January, he started packing his things for his move to me. In the back of his mind, he tried to picture what might fit into his car which he would drive out to me when the time was right. It was of course, uncomfortable for him being in the same house with Margaret, but his situation there was certainly not volatile like mine had been with David. He told me that they had both gone to a lawyer and started to make arrangements for their divorce.

Margaret was planning to have their children and their families over to their home for Easter dinner in April and Margaret had asked Eddie if he could tell the children after that. He agreed. It would give him time to help clean up their house and to sort through his things.

There are many consequences to divorce. Financial issues are big.

When I left David, we were already behind on our mortgage payments. David was so unsettled for the last couple of years of our marriage that he couldn't seem to keep any one job for any length of time. He went from job to job and there was much down time in between positions that put even more strain on our marriage, both financially and mentally.

He had been without a job so much of the time that the financial pressures were enormous. To stay afloat for many months while I was still there, I had resorted to over using credit cards to get by. I wasn't aware either that David just decided after I left to give up on the mortgage payments and to allow the chips to fall where they may.

After I left David and after many months of bill collectors calling me day and night, I had no choice but to file a personal bankruptcy. It was a huge relief to do this and it was just another way for me to get a fresh new start in my life.

My life was changing in a big way, in many wonderful ways.

Eddie and I talked on the phone and we decided to start looking at places for rent in my area. My sister's neighbor was a real estate agent and when I inquired, I was very happy to realize that she could help us find a nice place to rent. She was more than happy to help me out; we drove around together looking at places. Peggy and I actually became friends as I gushed to her about this wonderful man that I was starting a new life with.

It was a very exciting time for us; we would look at websites together, Eddie on his computer in NY and me on mine at my sister's. The anticipation of our time together in our own place was overwhelming in such a wonderful way.

Before we knew it, it was time for our February visit. Everything was right with the world when I was with Eddie. When we were alone in our hotel room, the world outside could disappear and we'd never know it. It didn't matter; all that mattered was that we were together.

When Eddie looked at me with those beautiful blue eyes of his, I melted; I still do. Oh, what he does to me.

As he kissed me that night, my mind went blank, except for him and his touch. He bent over just a bit so that I didn't have to stand on my tip toes to kiss him. He sighed as he told me how much he wanted me. I loved him so much.

He held my face in both his hands and said so gently, "Karen, are you listening to me? I love you, I love you, I love you. I love you more than I can say; is there a word that means more? I wish I knew what it was."

He stood behind me then and I could feel his warm sweet breath on my neck as he wrapped his arms around me.

As his hands moved up my body, he said, "I love everything about you. I love everything about your body."

My whole body tingled as his hands moved down the front of me until they were caressing my thighs. I turned to face him and held him tight. I loved to feel his huge shoulders and strong upper arms. My hands slid down his body now until he shuddered with anticipation of what was to come. And we both knew that what was to come was like paradise. Every time that we made love now was more pleasurable than the time before.

Such an intimate connection I had never felt. It was so gentle sometimes and at other times, we were like animals; not able to get enough of each other

Afterwards, we devoured some of the home-cooked food that I had so enjoyed preparing for him. He loved it! It felt like we were a married couple; only better. It felt like we were on an eternal honeymoon.

Knowing that Eddie would be back more permanently next month did not make it any easier to say good bye to him a few days later. He was an extension of me now and parting was always difficult, to say the least. I know that he felt the same way as I dropped him at the airport, when I saw the tears in his eyes.

About a week after Eddie went back in February, I found the perfect house for us to rent! It was a bit of an older home, not the kind I'd been used to living in as of late but I just loved it. It had such character. The neighborhood seemed so serene and quiet. The house had a huge backyard with fruit trees to the right and some Evergreens to the left as you looked out the patio doors. There was a nice sized wooden deck attached to the back of the house; it needed a bit of a sprucing up but I looked forward to working on that with Eddie. When I visited the home with Peggy, I took close to one hundred pictures that I later emailed to Eddie.

When Eddie saw all the pictures that I'd sent him, he loved it!

I couldn't help the enthusiasm in my voice.

"You are going to love it Eddie! The first time I saw it, it was raining out and I didn't get a real sense of the whole place. This time the sun was shining and I went out into the backyard! It's huge and beautiful with a fire pit and lots of room for gardens for flowers and vegetables. And the inside of the house is perfect. Just the right size for the two of us!"

I could just tell he was smiling when he said, "I love the excitement that I hear in your voice!"

"I can picture the two of us here together in OUR place, I am so excited!"

"Then what choice do we have," he said with a laugh, "Tell the landlord that we'll take it!"

Eddie was so anxious to make me more comfortable and the prospect of being back in a place of my own was very exciting.

So I signed the lease with the landlord and we faxed the same to Eddie for his signature. The landlord had agreed that the paperwork would be absolutely final on Eddie's approval when he was able to see the place in person on his next visit. Our lease agreement would officially begin on April 1st but the landlord offered to give us the keys a couple of weeks early which would work out perfect.

Eddie arrived for his next visit the second week of March. When I picked him up at the airport, I was surprised to see a real domestic side of him.

He said, "I have a great coupon for a huge discount at a housewares store, let's go shopping right now! We can get everything we need for our new place, everything to make you cozy."

"You want to go right now?" I said.

"Yes," said Eddie.

So off we went to the shopping mall.

We had such fun doing it too. I'd always done my shopping alone before so it was fun to have him with me and we laughed as our shopping cart almost toppled over several times because we had piled so much stuff into it.

Shopping before we even had time to make love was like foreplay to us. Brushing up against him as we shopped, smelling him, smiling at him, kissing him without being able to touch him where I really wanted to...........all those things made the anticipation even more exhilarating. We packed up all of our new purchases into my van.

We had hotel reservations, like we had in the past, so we drove there and checked in and reacquainted ourselves with the euphoria which was ours whenever we were together, at last. I felt like I'd waited forever to be with him again. We devoured each other until we were exhausted and satisfied for the moment.

When we got up the next morning, we had an appointment with our new landlord to pick up our keys at our new home. I was so excited for Eddie to see the place in person and just as I suspected, he loved everything about it.

He said, "I had no doubt that I would love the place as much as you. I want you to have whatever makes you happy baby. All I want to do is make you happy. You deserve it."

I could feel such respect from Eddie. He really valued my opinion, it was something I'd never felt with David.

The house had three bedrooms; ours over-looked the spacious backyard. It had two bathrooms; one was connected to our bedroom and the other was downstairs, outside the family room that had a huge wall covered in brick that outlined the fireplace. I was sure that as Eddie looked at that fireplace, he envisioned some very romantic moments in front of it, just the two of us, the same way that I did. We were ecstatic, to say the least.

So we wasted no time and as soon as we had the keys, we unloaded the van of all the purchases we had made the day previous, and went to the storage unit and started unloading all my things that had been kept there since I moved out of my last home with David. We were able to empty almost everything in a few trips, except for a couch that was too heavy for me to help him with.

After a long day of moving, we went back to the hotel room to relax and to eat and to make love and to sleep. We decided that we would check out of the hotel the following morning as we had made our new place livable enough to stay there from now on.

Eddie could stay with me for about a week before he had to go back to Long Island but he felt better knowing that I was now in "OUR" place and would have the comforts that he wanted me to have especially in his absence. Our first week together was dream-like. I could hardly believe that we were together in our own place; it was wonderful to say the least.

From the minute we walked into the house, Eddie had his toolbox out. He was fixing any little thing that needed it. It's funny to think now, my father was the kind of man who could do anything around the house and I assumed as a young woman that every man was made that way.

When I married David, I realized how wrong I was. Every project, no matter how big or small, became a major catastrophe, until I realized that it would be easier to call a professional in to take care of any household thing that needed to be done or to do it myself!

Now here was Eddie who seemed to be able to do anything around the house. I don't know; there is something about a man like that, that turns me on completely. A man who is good with his hands gets my vote every time!

I hated for Eddie to leave but I knew he had business to take care of in Long Island in order to come back to me permanently. His plan was to go back for a couple of days, to get a few things taken care of and to pack up his car with as many belongings as he could fit for the trip back to our new home.

Eddie had purchased a ticket for me to fly out to him, just three days later. It was a sunny day when I arrived there and we laughed as I saw how packed his car was, waiting there for us as we walked out of the terminal, hand in hand. We decided we would have some lunch locally and then we would head to "OUR" place. We drove about half way into the evening and decided to stop at a hotel for the night and to do the rest of the drive the following day. I had been up early to catch my flight and I was tired and needed a shower and a cozy bed and my Eddie close to me to snuggle with and to rest for a few hours.

T W E L V E

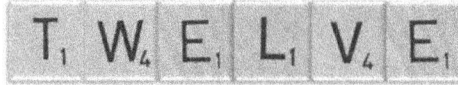

W E HEADED OUT EARLY the next day, fresh and anxious to get "HOME." The second half of the ride took about six hours. It was so good to get home. I went racing to the front door as Eddie started to unload the car. I was just so happy to be there with him!

Eddie called me from the front door to show me something.

He said, "Did you see this?"

I had no idea what he was talking about and was so surprised to see that to the right of our front door leading into the house was a beautiful wreath hanging on the brick wall. I don't know how I had missed it when I first went into the house, so intent was I in getting back.

I said, "Where did that come from? It wasn't there when I left here."

The wreath was made up of Spring-like greenery with ribbons of purple and green which are my favorite colors. It was such a welcoming decoration, such a nice home warming kind of gift. And my mouth dropped open in shock when I saw that it had several butterflies on it! "On the Wings of a Butterfly", one of our favorite songs and so meaningful to both of us.

I was in awe, as we looked further in the garden in front of the house and saw that there were large butterfly ornaments in the soil where I'd be planting flowers.

"Look at these butterflies in the front garden! Oh my gosh, where did they come from?" I said.

"I'm as baffled as you," said Eddie.

As we walked back into the yard, we saw that every fruit tree had a large ornamental butterfly on it.

At first I looked to Eddie and I could see that he was just as surprised as I! I was moved to tears. I mean I was sobbing. I was so incredibly touched by the thought of someone bestowing us with such a meaningful gesture. It meant so much to us. It took a while for both of us to compose ourselves enough to even begin to think who might have done this for us.

I phoned both my daughters to ask them if they were aware of what was left at our house.

My younger daughter said, "Gee mom, I wish that I could take the credit for that but I have no idea who might have done that for you. It is incredibly thoughtful."

Then I called my sister Nancy who told me that she and Peggy had rushed over there earlier in the day to beat us home and to leave these wonderful gifts around the outside of our new place to welcome us home.

I could not have imagined a more moving gift. I cried as I thanked Nancy and told her just how much her gesture meant to me and Eddie both.

I called Peggy then and thanked her too.

They both knew the significance of the butterfly to us.

It is a moment, etched in my mind that I will never forget.

One of my favorite quotes came to my mind in that moment. "Life is not measured by the number of breaths that we take, but by the moments that take our breath away!" And this was truly one of those moments.

Never before in my life had I experienced the kind of emotion that I was feeling with Eddie and every part of our lives together. I shook my head in disbelief then, as I still do oftentimes, marveling at what my life has become. It was as if all the years that were spent unhappily were melting away with every new moment I spent with Eddie.

The next couple of weeks were the best I'd experienced yet with Eddie. We got settled in, working on the house to make it our own.

Eddie and I both enjoyed decorating a home, including painting the walls. He had done painting for years as a hobby and as a supplemental income. I had painted my previous homes as well. It was such a pleasant reality for me to learn that when it came to working on a project together, we automatically worked in such harmony.

When we decided which room we would paint first, it really came as no surprise as we just picked up the rollers and brushes and just jumped right in there each doing our own part, with hardly a word of explanation to each other. It felt like this whole relationship was meant to be! We were so connected, in every aspect of our lives thus far, like we were one whole person being together. I'd never felt anything that resembled what I had with Eddie.

The day of finalizing my divorce had finally arrived and I was very happy that Eddie was here to support me. He was taking such good care of me in every way possible. I couldn't take him to the courthouse with me because I didn't want to cause a confrontation with David but just knowing that he would be there for me when I returned home was enough to get me through my court appearance. Nancy had agreed to go with me so I wouldn't be alone.

It was probably the most bizarre moment in my life yet, it felt so strange to be there. As I waited with Nancy outside the courthouse, I shivered from the cold wind that whipped past us or was it my nerves? There was a long line of people in front of us and behind us waiting just as we were, to get inside. Part of me wondered if David would show up and follow through with this divorce to its finality.

I said to Nancy, "What if he doesn't show up to finish this today, I don't know what I'll do."

She said, "He will be here, I'm watching for him."

I just wanted it to finally be over. I never wavered; I knew that I had to do it. It was the final step to my freedom!

Right before the courthouse doors opened to the public for the start of their day, Nancy whispered quietly, "I see him, and he's at the end of the line. He's here, it's okay Karen, this will be done today."

I was relieved as we walked inside, shaky but relieved. I never looked back as we walked inside the building and went through security and then to the appointed room.

My lawyer had given me a brief description of himself; we had conducted all our business up to this point, on the phone and through email and when I didn't see him there at first, I wondered if I would in fact, get the closure today that I had hoped for. Never having been in court for too many things before in my lifetime, I soon realized that it's pretty much the norm for lawyers to keep their clients and the judges, as well, waiting.

When Nancy and I walked into the courtroom, there were already a few lawyers and their clients there. We sat down on one side of the room and as we whispered between ourselves David walked in and after glancing my way once, he sat down on the other side of the room.

The judge was announced and then he had a seat at the head of the room.

The judge said, "If there is any lawyer with his client who is ready to go, please come forward now."

A couple of cases went ahead in front of the judge to be heard.

Since I was not ready, I got up and walked out into the hall and was greeted by my lawyer. I sighed with relief as he explained to me what I could expect when I was in front of the judge.

When our turn came, David and I stood on either side of the lawyer. My lawyer read off all of the statements that David and I had previously agreed to.

The judge asked, "Are all these statements that your lawyer has stated, in fact, true?"

David and I both said, "Yes."

"Then I will grant this divorce to you both in the state of Illinois on this first day of April."

I remember having laughed at the irony when my lawyer had first told me that the finalization of my divorce would be on April Fool's Day!

And so it was done! I'll never forget the moments that followed.

As I walked out of the court room, there was David, in the middle of a crowd of people, looking so awkward. All I could see was him. It was like there was just a blur of color around him as the crowds of people moved past us. There was noise and there were colors. And there was David..............all alone; he looked so lost. My heart was breaking for him, even after all the years of hell I'd been through with him and because of him. I was still feeling so sad for him and for me. We had invested so many years in each other, almost forty years to be exact.

I asked Nancy quietly, "What should I do? Should I say something to him?"

I'm so glad she was there with me to help me. She said, "NO! Don't!"

And as she grabbed my arm for support, she touched David's shoulder as we walked past him and we quickly retired to the ladies room so that I wouldn't have to look at him again.

I cried when we got there, just so happy to be out of his sight and we stayed there long enough to know that he must surely be gone from the building now. I did not want to risk having to look at him once more that day. I wasn't sure if my heart could take it.

As we walked outside into the sunshine of the day now, I took a huge breath of fresh air and all of a sudden felt like my chest would burst with gladness. I was so proud of myself for following through with what I knew had to be done and what I realize now was probably the most difficult thing I'd ever had to do.

I said to Nancy, "I've never felt such relief in my life before! I did it!"

She hugged me saying, "I'm so proud of you and I'm so happy for you, I love you sis."

I never thought that I'd have the courage to divorce David. For many years I'd seen divorce happen to other people. I never thought that it would become a part of my life and until it happens to you, you just don't realize how overwhelming it is. It touches you at your core. It changes you as a person, forever. And for me it was a good and wonderful change and a new beginning.

And to celebrate that new beginning, Nancy and I went and picked up Eddie at our house and we all headed out for a late celebratory breakfast!

We drank Mimosas with our meal.

Eddie toasted, "To you Karen and your new found freedom!"

Nancy toasted, "To you Karen and to Eddie and to your new lives together!"

I toasted too, "To you Nancy, thank you for always being there for me, I don't know what I'd do without you, thanks for all your support!"

T H I R T E E N

THE NEXT COUPLE OF weeks were filled with wonderful things that made up my new reality with Eddie. I had to pinch myself sometimes, realizing how my life had changed and how fulfilling and peaceful it had become. I could hardly believe how special it felt to be happy every single day.

My children first met Eddie when they had us over for dinner. It was awkward for just a few short moments when we first walked in to their place but Eddie just exudes such kindness with his smile and with his eyes that we were all comfortable together quickly. I could tell by the way that my children looked at us that they liked him. They could see the way that we looked at each other. They could see the way we smiled at each other. They couldn't help but be happy for us. Everyone loves to ask Eddie questions about what it was like to be NY city cop and my kids were no exception so we didn't lack for conversation for even a moment.

I come from a big family with three sisters and two brothers and we are a very close-knit family and ever since I had left David, all of my siblings had been concerned for my happiness and welfare. In fact, before Eddie moved to be with me, my oldest brother, Ken, took me out to lunch to "pump me for information."

He said, "So tell me about this guy. How do you know that you can trust him?"

I laughed when I told him, "All I can tell you is how safe and loved he makes me feel."

This lunch with Ken took place while I was planning one of my trips to New York, before my brother had met Eddie.

When I told Ken that I was going, he was very concerned for me.

He said, "You may feel like you can trust him but I'm concerned for your safety, going to another state by yourself to meet him. What if I asked you to get a copy of Eddie's driver's license so that I could double check on his background?"

I said, "I'll ask him. I think that he would be fine with that."

In fact, later that day when I asked Eddie for a copy of his driver's license to pacify my brother, I was so pleased with his reply.

Eddie said, "I don't blame your brother. That's really nice that he's so concerned for you. I will go make a copy of my license for you right now and I'll overnight it to you."

It arrived at Nancy's house for me the very next day.

I laughed as I told Nancy, "I have a copy of Eddie's driver's license and I'll show you where it will be while I'm in New York. And if I end up missing, you will know where to find it and how to start your search for me in New York."

I never actually showed it to my brother or anyone else. There was never a need. I still have it.

So I held up for as long as I could but it finally came the time when I had to share Eddie. It was time for him to start meeting my other family members.

It felt incredible to introduce Eddie to all of them, including my older brother. I was so proud to stand next to Eddie and to call him my boyfriend. I could see by the looks on all of their faces as they met him, that they respected him from the first moment and were very interested to get to know him more. They could also see without doubt that this man treated me with respect and kindness.

We all got together for dinner one evening and as we waited in the foyer of the restaurant, a waitress passed by us with appetizers. Eddie reached for one with a napkin and very quickly handed both to me to serve me before himself.

My brother couldn't help but notice.

He said with a big grin on his face, "Wow Eddie, we have a lot to live up to here, don't we?"

In a very exaggerated way, he did the same then for his fiancée and handed her the appetizer that he had previously been prepared to put into his own mouth.

We all laughed then as my sister's husband followed suit!

While we sat at dinner, I could see how inquisitive my family was with all sorts of questions for Eddie. They asked him many questions about his job as a New York City Cop.

Nancy's husband asked, "So Eddie, where were you when the Twin Towers went down?"

Eddie went on to say, "I was actually off duty at the time and on the golf course with a few friends and when we were done with our game, we were surprised to see everyone in the clubhouse glued to what was happening on the TV screen. I was shocked, of course."

Everyone at the table was so curious to hear Eddie's stories.

I had become embarrassed, for a long time, at David's behavior and never knew what he might say to make himself look foolish. It was so different being with Eddie and it was wonderful.

When someone would ask me, "So do your kids like Eddie?" or "Did your brother like him?"

There was no hesitation in telling them that there was just nothing about Eddie that someone would not like! People liked everything about him. From the moment he opened his mouth, it was apparent that he was a kind and honest and smart man.

For the most part, Eddie and I spent most of our time alone. We relished our time alone. It felt great for a change to be selfish and just to do what felt right and good to me. We spent a lot of time, on my days off from work, just lingering in bed in the morning.

Eddie would whisper to me in the morning, "Stay right there, I'll be right back, I'll go start the coffee."

And then a couple of minutes later he would jump right back into bed with me to snuggle. Or if I woke up and he wasn't next to me, I would pick up my phone and text him.

I'd say something like, "Come n get me baby," or "Anyone wanna snuggle?"

I would laugh as I would hear him get up abruptly from wherever he was in the house, and he would come running up the stairs and burst into the room with a huge smile on his face.

He'd say, "I thought you'd never wake up! I missed you!"

Our mornings alone together were my favorite times with Eddie.

All that we had to do was look at each other, just look at each other and we would smile and then laugh, for no apparent reason, just because it felt so good to be together.

We'd get busy some days with painting or decorating our new place and I was so surprised to have this feeling of missing him. We might even be in the same room, but I would miss him. If I was not able to look into his eyes and focus on him totally, I missed him. Because that was all I ever wanted to do really. Just to gaze into his eyes and to hold his hand and to sit next to him and to feel his warmth next to me.

When we are together, the time always passes so quickly and before we knew it, it was time for Eddie to return to New York for Easter dinner as he had promised Margaret.

He said, "I don't want to go but I must. This will be the last time I have to go back."

I said, "I know, I'm not happy about it but I know that you have to go. I will miss you so much."

"I do feel better knowing that you are comfortable here now in our new place and you have everything you need here," Eddie said.

"Everything except you," I said.

It was so difficult for us to say goodbye, but on Thursday before Easter, Eddie got in his car and headed back to have dinner with his children and with Margaret one last time. He promised that he would be back after the holiday and after packing up his car with the rest of his things.

It was heart wrenching to say goodbye but we both knew that it had to be done and that we would be back together in about a week.

My kids all came to my house for Easter dinner. They are such good people, I couldn't help but have a nice time with them; all the while wondering how Eddie was doing.

The week dragged by. I went to work and came home to the empty house, happy to have my own space but longing for Eddie's arms around me. We talked on the phone several times a day but as the week wore on, I just wanted him back with me and could hardly stand the physical pain I felt yearning for him. I've never felt anything like that pain before in my life and when his trip back got delayed for one more miserable long day, I didn't think that I could live through it. I could hardly even speak to him on the phone, it was just too painful.

I remember it was a warm and sunny day and I just prayed for the strength to get through it. I couldn't talk to anyone. I was miserable and just absolutely certain that the only way that was going to change was when he came back to me. I sat out in my yard in the sun with my sunglasses on, the ones with the hearts on the arms. Those were the sunglasses I'd worn that first day that I'd met Eddie in person. I sat out in the sun and I cried and I got sunburn. I couldn't even eat that day.

Ever since my relationship had begun with Eddie, I wasn't able to eat like normal. I lost a lot of weight back then, I'd think about Eddie and totally lose track of time some days until it was dinner time.

I'd say to myself, "I don't think I ate today."

It's mind-boggling what "Being in Love" can do to you physically. It was all encompassing. It was my world.

I was totally unaware of what was going on in the news. Someone would ask me what I thought of this or that and I wouldn't have a clue as to what they were talking about. It was like a horse with blinders on. I couldn't see anything else and what's more it just didn't matter!

Eddie finally headed back to me late in the day that next Friday, after saying goodbye to his only sister and to his mother, not really knowing for sure when he might see them next. I think it may have been the very longest day of my life.

I finally exhausted myself in misery, went up to my room and fell fast asleep on the bed.

It was about three o'clock in the morning when Eddie whispered to me, "Karen...Karen...I'm here Karen."

With that my eyes opened and I could see that Eddie was kneeling on the floor next to me with tears in his eyes. At first I thought I might be dreaming but as I shook my head I realized that I was not.

I said, "Oh my God, I thought you'd never get here."

And while Eddie stayed on his knees he bent down to kiss me as I lay there and we kissed passionately.

I was holding him as he held me. He never even took off his jacket because we could not let go of each other. Eddie knelt on the floor there next to me for the next hour. We could hardly speak at first. We just held each other and we cried and we kissed.

I could hardly believe that he was back. He caressed my face as he spoke to me.

Eddie said, "I promise you here and now. I will never leave you alone again. I can't stand the thought of it. I missed you so much. I felt physically ill without you by my side."

"Oh my God, I missed you, anywhere we need to go, we will go together," I said.

We laughed then as Eddie tried to get up off the floor. He'd been kneeling there for an hour. That was after he'd been in his cramped car for the last twelve hours driving home to me.

I was supposed to work that next morning but there was no way that anyone could tear me away from his side that next day! I called in to let them know that I would not be in and fell asleep that morning in Eddie's arms. It was where I was supposed to be. It is where I am going to be all the days of my life.

The next morning, we took our time reacquainting ourselves with each other and stayed in bed late.

I had longed for his touch for what seemed like a month. Every time we made love it was like the first time again. We made love that morning until we felt satisfied and then we started over again like the first time had never happened; our desire was that strong. He feasted on me, we feasted on each other. The sounds that I made when he touched me surprise me still. I'm not sure where they come from but it's uncontrollable. Such satisfaction I've never felt. The passion between us was immeasurable.

We had a much deserved big breakfast when we finally managed to make our way downstairs.

Eddie promised again, "I will never travel without you again. Wherever I go, you are coming with me."

I said, "That sounds wonderful to me because, I can hardly breathe when we are apart."

I was shocked when I looked into Eddie's car to see the small space that was left in his car for him to sit in because of all the stuff he had packed. It was packed from the floor up to the ceiling.

He said, "I was so anxious to get back, I thought I'd never get here. I was speeding a bit and I got stopped by the police. Lucky for me he only gave me a warning but he too was marveling at how much I'd managed to fit into my car."

"I don't know how you drove like that all that way Eddie, it's so cramped!"

"I just didn't care," Eddie said, "All I could think of was getting back to you as fast as my car would drive me."

I helped him to unpack his car. We moved his things into the house and into the garage. Eddie was here for good now.

I got spoiled pretty quickly with all the kind and thoughtful things that Eddie does for me. I've hardly washed a dish since he's been with me here.

He says, "It's the least that I can do for you when you prepare me such wonderful meals."

He makes me coffee every morning and brings it up to me while I'm getting ready for the day.

For the first couple of weeks once he came back, I drove back and forth to work until Eddie asked me if he could drive me.

He said, "I don't want you walking out in the cold or rainy weather, let me drive you to work, ok?"

"That would be really sweet Eddie, I don't even have to think about where I'll park anymore."

I loved the idea of being pampered that way. And to top it off, he decided to start preparing my lunch for me every work day. My eyes filled with tears when I opened my lunch in the break room at work and realized that he had put a love note into my lunch.

He'd write things like, "Love is taking you to work when it's snowing out and you don't have to walk in it. I Love You. Eddie."

Or, "Please love me forever."

And, "My Dear, you are a sight for sore eyes in the morning and at noon and at night, I Love you."

And still, "You are my everything."

There has been a new one in my lunch every day since that first time. I have saved every one of them. Perhaps I'll put them into an album of sorts. I will keep them forever no doubt.

My life with Eddie is idyllic. Surely, my life with him is the closest that I will ever get to Paradise right here on Earth. I've made him promise me that he will take extra good care of his health because I need him to live for a very long time with me.

When we watch TV at night together, he makes sure that I am comfy and warm, wrapping a blanket around me when needed. If I get up to get something, he's right there when I come back ready to cover me up again. If I have cold feet that don't seem to warm up quick enough with the touch of his gentle hands, as I laugh till I cry, he lifts up his shirt and places my feet right on his warm skin so as to warm them up quicker. He is my Knight in Shining Armor.

He brings my coffee to me every day without fail and makes my breakfast. Never before have I been treated with such care.

When we have family over at our house or when we go to someone else's place, we love them all dearly but can hardly wait to be alone again, to be able to kiss and hug and touch each other at whim. I can be in the same room with him and feel like I miss him when we aren't totally concentrating on one another.

I'm reminded of some verse I'd heard in a song that so impressed me and so applied to my life as it changed so immensely.

The song says "not to cling to your fears. You can't buy back wasted time, life is so short. So stop and love and dance and live and laugh until you cry. Don't you wake up and realize that your life has passed you by. To your heart and your soul you must be true."

Wiser words I've never known. It feels so good now to live with no regrets and to live every day like it's my last.

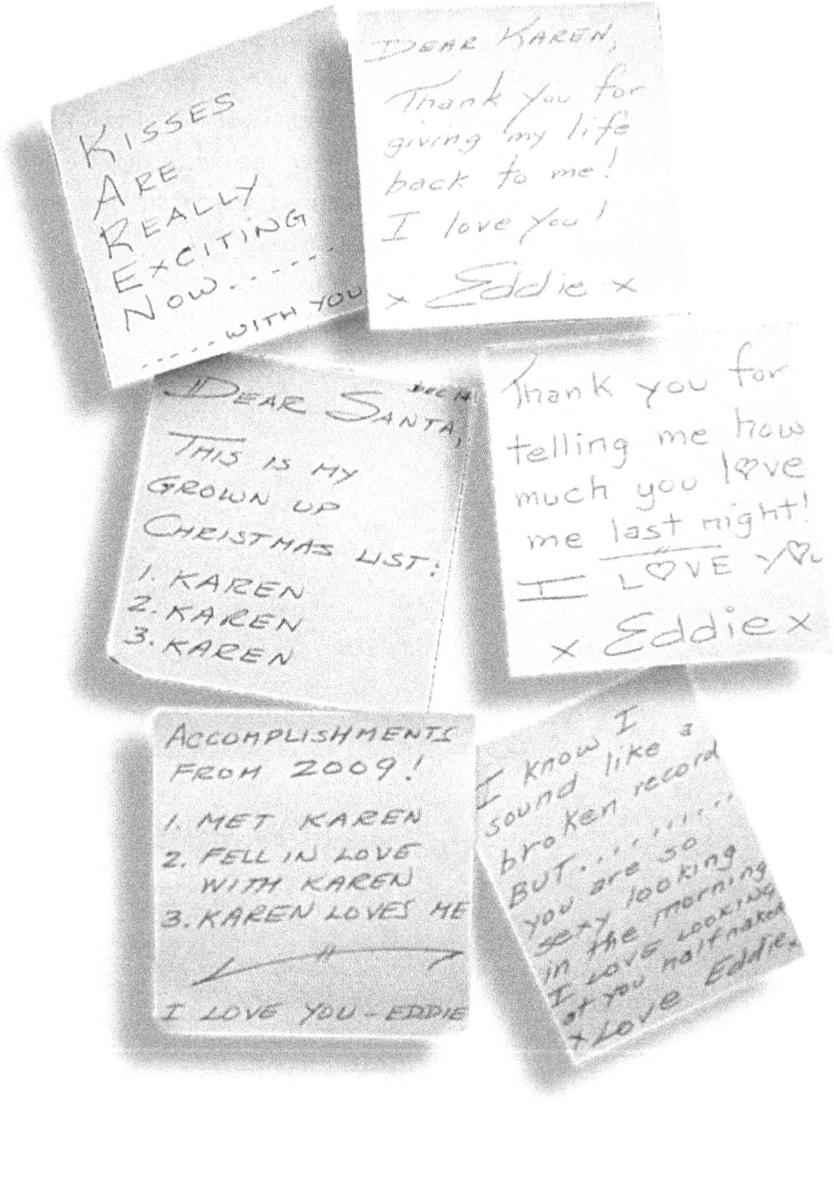
KISSES
ARE
REALLY
EXCITING
NOW.......
.....WITH YOU
DEAR KAREN,
Thank you for
giving my life
back to me!
I love you!
x Eddie x
DEAR SANTA,
THIS IS MY
GROWN UP
CHRISTMAS LIST:
1. KAREN
2. KAREN
3. KAREN
Thank you for
telling me how
much you love
me last night!
I LOVE YOU
x Eddie x
ACCOMPLISHMENTS
FROM 2009!
1. MET KAREN
2. FELL IN LOVE
WITH KAREN
3. KAREN LOVES ME
I LOVE YOU - EDDIE
I know I
sound like a
broken record
BUT.........
you are so
sexy looking
in the morning
I love looking
at you half naked
x Love Eddie x

F O U R T E E N

IT'S BEEN ONE YEAR since I began to write this love story.

Our lives are as calm and peaceful and loving as they can possibly be. My children are doing remarkably well. I couldn't ask for more; they are all successful in their careers and their personal lives. I have such respect for each of them. I believe that all of us are so much better off because of my divorcing David, even David. He has to take care of himself now and try to make his way in this world, however he chooses.

I ended up leaving my job at the hospital. It became a verbally abusive situation which I realized as time went by and I became healthier in my head. I realized that I'd gone right from an abusive marriage to an abusive kind of job and I realize now that no job is worth that. This life here is so short and I'm going to enjoy every day to the fullest and spend my time doing things that make me feel happy and fulfilled.

When I was getting frustrated at my job, Eddie was right there to support me.

He said, "I don't like how that job makes you feel. I don't like what it's doing to you. I will support you no matter what you decide to do."

I told him, "I'm so grateful for your support. It means so much to me that you want what's best for me."

We love spending all of our time together. We feel so lucky to have found each other.

Eddie and I became engaged this past March 1st. He got down on one knee and professed his undying love for me.

He said, "I promise to woo you forever and to treat you like a queen, so that you never change your mind about me. I love you with all of my heart Karen; please say that you will marry me. Please be my wife."

I said, "How can I resist you my love? Of course I will marry you."

We both cried as we hugged and cherished the moment.

It's summertime now as we are planning our wedding. It will be in our spacious backyard alongside our beautiful garden.

I can picture it now.

We will walk out of our patio door onto our deck which will be covered with purple flowers. There will be romantic music playing as we walk down the center of the yard through the open tent which will be full of our family and close friends. And at the end of the tent we will stand with the preacher in front of my garden as we profess our love and devotion to each other in front of God and all who are present. We will celebrate with good friends and good food and good music. We will dance the night away under the stars until we cannot dance any longer.

As I look at my garden now, I realize again what an incredible reflection it is of my life with Eddie.

He made my garden even larger this year to accommodate more of the herbs that I love to cook with. It's magical as I water them with the hose in the sunshine. I can see the magnificent hues of the rainbow in the light mist of the water as it sprays my flowers and vegetables.

My eyes blur with tears at the beauty of the garden, and as I think about the wonderfully happy life that I am so lucky to be living now. I feel incredibly blessed.

On the flower side of my garden, I'd planted a sea of Irises last summer.

And there they stand as they have multiplied and thrived in their purple majesty. And right there at the edge of the flowers is one lone Iris that I've never seen before. I can't even tell what color it will be but there is no question that it's different than all the rest.

I can't wait for it to open to see what color it will be; the buds are almost black. I don't know if it will be a deeper purple or if it might be blue.

I do know that it will open exactly when it's time.

Just like all the new experiences that are in store for me and Eddie. I can hardly wait for each new day with him.

Every time I think that I can't love him anymore than I already do, he does something to make me change my mind. And I am in awe of the depth of emotion that I feel.

WHAT A
GREAT
WEEKEND!!
I LOVE YOU
× EDDIE ×

Love Is.....
Being there
for you
always!
× Eddie ×

YOU
are Too beautiful
for
words!

Love, Eddie
× × ×

You Know I
want you------
You know you
want meeee---

I L♥ve
You!

You Are
My SPECIAL
ANGEL!

Dear Karen
I can't
believe it, but
it's been 2yrs
since we met.
I fall in love
with you MORE
each day.
I L♥VE YOU!
× Eddie ×

E P I L O G U E

THE WEDDING (S)

I'M SUCH A LUCKY girl. I've married Eddie twice so far.

The minute his Divorce Papers were finalized after many months of sitting in a pile in the Courthouse in New York, we couldn't wait to get married. In fact, we planned a trip to New York knowing that the papers would be ready for pick up. We didn't trust the mail or the lawyers to get it right. We drove to the Courthouse ourselves to pick them up. That was such a joyful ride. We were so excited to finally know that we could become Mr. and Mrs.

Once we left the Courthouse with the legal paperwork, we actually stopped on the side of the Highway so that I could capture the moment with my camera. I have a little movie of us.

Eddie is holding up the papers and he says, "The Courts finally came through for us baby! Here they are. I'm free at last, free to marry you!"

I moved the camera back and forth from his face to mine as we were screaming and yelling with joy. Finally, I could be Eddie's wife. Finally we could shout it from the rooftops. I'm with him and he's with me!

We'd both been dreaming about it for months.

On our way back to Eddie's sister's place where we usually stay when we visit New York frequently, we stopped at Jones Beach. It's one of our favorite places in the world, especially in the colder weather when it's deserted. It's our beach. We go there often. The view is spectacular, the infinite ocean and the sand, spectacular.

This day Eddie stands behind me with his arms wrapped around me as we face the ocean. I love the sounds as the waves crash into the beach. I close my eyes and I can feel the unmistakable presence of a power greater than myself. It's the power that led me to Eddie in the first place.

"Life is incredible, isn't Eddie?" I say as I feel the wind blowing through my hair.

"More incredible than I ever thought possible baby," Eddie says.

While we were still in New York, I phoned a friend of my brothers who is a minister who performs Weddings to see what dates she would be available to perform a second Wedding, which we started to plan even before the first was done.

When we got home from NY, I phoned my kids and said, "Eddie and I are getting married next week. Can you be there?"

My son said, "Of course Mom, I wouldn't miss it."

My older daughter got all choked up as she said, "Yes mom, nothing could keep me from being there. I'm so happy for you both."

My youngest daughter had to be out of town but we decided to go ahead with it anyway, knowing that this would be our first of two celebrations.

Now we also swore the kids to secrecy. They were the only ones who knew that we were going to the Courthouse to marry. We wanted to surprise everyone else with an Announcement in the mail which would include an Invite to the "Dream Wedding" where we would do it again with all our family and friends as witnesses. It was so much fun to do it this way.

I did tell my sister Nancy that we had picked up the Official Divorce Papers.

She said, "Oh my God, you didn't get married in New York, did you?"

I said coyly, "No."

Nancy said, "Well what's your plan? I'm so excited for you. Tell me, tell me please."

As I laughed out loud, I said, "I'm sorry, I can't do that. You will know soon what's happening. Please don't ask me anymore, okay?"

"All right," she said sounding defeated, "I won't ask any more questions."

The day after we had returned home Ed and I went to get our Marriage License. The clerk there had us raise our right hands and swear that the information we were giving was true and complete to the best of our knowledge. With License in hand we were ready.

Ed and I were both curious to see what a Courthouse Wedding would be like. The next week came and my daughter came to our house to drive with us to the Courthouse. It was such a beautiful summer day that before we left our house, we went out to the backyard to take some pictures.

We have a beautiful Orchard on one side of our huge yard. There are two Apple trees and one Pear. Attached to each tree is a large colorful butterfly that's been there since Eddie first moved here with me. Some of my favorite pictures from that day are in front of those trees; just me and Ed and the Butterflies.

My son met us out front of the Courthouse.

As he gave me a big hug, he said, "I'm so happy for you mom. I love you."

As we entered the building, we went through Security, as is the norm for a government building. I left my camera and my phone in the car, knowing from past experience that those were not allowed here.

We were directed to the Court cashier to pay a fee and then we were instructed to have a seat in the Hall while it was decided who would perform the Ceremony for us and in which Court Room it would take place.

We were pleasantly surprised when we walked into the room where the Wedding would take place and realized that we were the only couple getting married that morning.

Judge Joseph Polito greeted us all warmly with a smile and a handshake. He congratulated us and asked us if we would be taking pictures.

I said, "I thought that you couldn't bring a camera in here."

He said, "They should really tell you that when you come here to get married, you can absolutely take pictures."

So with that I asked my daughter to run out to the car to bring the camera in. When she came back in, Eddie and I faced each other and held hands as we looked into each other's eyes.

The Judge began, "We are gathered here today to join this man and this woman in the holy bonds of Matrimony..."

I couldn't believe that we were finally here. I have to admit that some of the words are a blur now, it happened so quickly.

Before I knew it I was saying, "I do."

After Eddie repeated the same, the Judge pronounced us Husband and Wife and said, "You may kiss the Bride."

We kissed with tears in our eyes as the Judge and my son and daughter clapped and it was done. It was beautiful and simple.

As we left the room, I said to Eddie, "Are we married? What just happened? It went by in a blur, am I really your wife?"

He said, "Yes baby, you are. You are my wife and I am your husband and I love you more than words can say."

After taking a few more photos in front of the Courthouse, the four of us drove together to a quaint Irish Restaurant to celebrate with drinks and lunch. Both of the kids had to go to work after that.

Eddie and I stopped at home and then went to a Photo Studio where we had made an appointment to have some Professional photos done to commemorate the day.

The photographer asked, "What are you two celebrating today?"

Eddie said, "I was lucky enough to marry this beautiful woman today."

She said, "Aww, that's so sweet, Congratulations to both of you."

We laughed and we kissed as she snapped pictures of us together, some serious, some not so much. One of my favorite photos from there is the one where I'm standing behind Eddie with my arms wrapped loosely around his neck. He is holding my hands with his. You can see our wedding rings; such a beautiful symbol of our love and how we are wrapped up in our love for each other.

When we returned home, we just sat down and relaxed with more Champagne and talked about how wonderful the day was, from start to finish.

When we went to bed together that night, it was different. It was better. I didn't think that was possible but it was even better than it had ever been before.

As we lay together, wrapped in each other's arms, Eddie said, "I am so proud to be your husband. Thank you for marrying me today. I will not disappoint you."

The next day when we got up, the planning began. We worked on a mailing list of people who would be so happy for us once they heard the great news of our Union.

We chose the date for the next Celebration to be two months to the day after the Courthouse Wedding. I had eight weeks to put it together and I loved every moment of the planning. It was to be our Dream Wedding.

We designed an Announcement/Invitation that read, "WE DID IT, WE GOT MARRIED! You're invited to join us as we Pledge our Vows and Rejoice in our Love with Family and Friends. We will Eat and Drink and Dance under the stars."

It then gave the date and time and place for the party. There was no question that it would be in our beautiful backyard just like we had hoped.

There was a lot to do. I called a Party Tent Rental that I had used in the past to order a beautiful huge tent for the yard that would accommodate all of our guests.

We made an appointment with a florist so that I could carry a Bouquet down the aisle. I wanted my two daughters who would walk before me to carry flowers as well. We ordered boutonnieres for Eddie and for my son.

We ordered a special cake, bought party supplies and drinks.

I emailed back and forth with the Minister to go over the Ceremony that she had planned and to make some changes and additions to the Vows we would recite to each other. My sister agreed to be our Photographer.

We found a DJ; music and dancing an absolute essential in our plans. We planned the music for the ceremony and for dancing.

It was just a bit nerve wracking as the date drew near. I was addicted to the weather websites every day. The weather looked very precarious with lots of rain and wind for several days before the wedding and I just kept praying that the weather would cooperate. I just kept hoping that as the day drew nearer, that the weather prediction would become more favorable.

Eddie and I both were waking in the middle of the night; our minds were so full of details and we were just so anxious to experience this next Ceremony. We both wanted everything to be perfect and we were determined to do everything possible to make that happen.

The courthouse wedding was nice but we knew this one coming up would be even more joyful.

There were so many people in my life that had been so genuinely excited and interested in me and my unexpected courtship with Eddie. It was my dream to gather up all these people in one place who had been so supportive of me. These were the people who wanted all the details of every time Eddie and I would be together. These were the people who were so happy for us, so happy to hear our love story and how it progressed. These were the people who hugged me when they saw the tears in my eyes when I was missing Eddie so much when he was still in New York.

Our happiness was like a magnet, people were so drawn to our story. It made people around us happy to be reminded of what true love is. This next celebration was the zenith of our love.

I watched them put up the tent the day before the Wedding. I couldn't believe how they could put up such a huge tent in such a short amount of time. They battled the wind just a bit but it was supposed to be dying down by the next day, I hoped.

From just a few plastic pipes strewn on the ground, I was amazed at the process of completing this set up. The roof of the tent was laid on the ground, attached to the connected pipes and then raised to its majestic eighteen foot peak. We then decided to put up a few sidewalls on this hexagon shaped tent in case of rain and to cut the wind if it was still around the next day. We left two sides wide open. We would stand at one of the open sides for the ceremony with huge pine trees opposite the orchard to be our backdrop. The sidewalls had windows and once I walked inside the tent, I knew we had made the right choice. It was exactly the right feel for this party...it was perfect.

We had to decide next exactly where the DJ would set up so that we could put the dance floor in place. After the installation people left, Eddie and I looked out into the yard in awe. There was par lighting attached inside the peak of the tent. We turned the lights on then because it was getting dark out and just smiled to see how awesome it looked.

I said to Eddie, "Let's try out the dance floor, yes?"

He said, "Sure," as he ran to it and started boogey-ing like there was no tomorrow.

I laughed so hard, I could hardly hold the camera still to take a few photos of the tent and of Eddie.

And then he got serious. He said, "Put down that camera woman and get over here and dance with me."

"Okay, you handsome man."

I hummed to Eddie what our first song would be as we rehearsed our first dance for the next night.

"It's really going to happen tomorrow Eddie, isn't it?"

"Yes baby, it is."

The day arrived and we were ecstatic that there were no clouds in the sky. And it couldn't have been any bluer. It was a little cool but such a beautiful day.

We were up early of course in anticipation of the day. We set to work right away and started setting up the tables where people would sit once the Ceremony was over. On the side of the tent where we would recite our vows is where we set up the chairs now. We set them up in perfect rows on two sides with an aisle down the middle for me to walk.

We attached white tablecloths to each table so that they would not blow away. We set up the banquet tables for the food and for the cake. The rest would have to be done closer to the guests' arrival because of the wind.

As we made preparations inside the house, the doorbell rang. One of our guests wanted to drop something off early for the party. Our friend had two large beautiful Mum plants in her arms.

For several weeks before the party, many of the guests had been asking what they could do to help or what they could bring. So being that it was soon to be Fall and being that my favorite color is purple and being that the whole color scheme of the wedding was white and purple, I had told those guests that I would love it if they were to bring some purple Mums to help decorate the yard.

So here she was with the first two Mum plants.

I jumped into the shower and started to prepare myself for this day. I knew that people would be arriving early and I needed to look my best. I got dressed in a semi casual outfit for now. I wore a long sleeved purply blue blouse with a cute little skirt and sandals. My plan was to begin greeting the guests as they arrived and then to sneak off to my room with my daughters to dress for the Ceremony.

When I was ready to go, I noticed in the yard that someone had placed another half a dozen Mum plants on the stairs of the deck right outside my patio doors, which I would walk right by on my way down the aisle to Eddie. They looked perfect. We ended up with a total of twelve Mums decorating the whole area.

I noticed too, that as promised, my sister had made sure that there were supplies in the yard ready to start a huge bonfire in our fire pit which we thought would make the party even more cozy.

Eddie had several errands to do for me too. He had a cake to pick up and ice for drinks.

More importantly I was so happy for him that his sister from New York along with her husband had arrived the night before to join us for our Wedding. They were staying in a nearby Hotel and he was going to pick them up as well.

My daughters arrived early to make appetizers and to assist me with all the preparations. I had also hired a couple of helpers to assist with the food and the cake and the cleanup. I had made a list of all the things that they could do for me to make the party run smoothly.

My sister arrived and started snapping photos right away.

As I showed the helpers where the sugar for coffee was, I spilled sugar all over the place and as we all laughed my daughter told me, "Mom, back away from the sugar, we will take care of everything here. Go greet your guests."

My other daughter said, "Maybe you need a shot to calm you down."

I laughed and said, "It probably wouldn't be a bad idea."

So with that she pulled a bottle of vodka out of the freezer and I gulped a big sip down just like that! We all laughed like moms and daughters and friends do just because.

As I went over the list with them, Eddie came down all dressed and ready to go. He looked incredible in his navy suit and his purple shirt and tie. And oh my, he smelled so good. I couldn't wait to get my hands on him.

Everyone started arriving now. The guests were finding their way to the yard and to their seats in anticipation of the Ceremony. Eddie and I were greeting everyone with such joy.

The minister was here. Sonja knew exactly what she was doing. You could tell she had lots of experience dealing with nervous wedding participants.

Right before I went upstairs with my daughters to change, I looked out into the yard through the patio doors to see the results of what I had planned and it was good. It was incredible really, it had all come together, even better than I'd hoped.

The white tent looked even whiter against the cloudless blue sky. There were, by this time, forty or so people milling around, drinking, talking and laughing, inside the tent. You could feel the atmosphere was that of pure joy.

Through the windows of the tent, you could see my garden and the fruit trees which were still rich with foliage. More Purple Mums had appeared and were scattered all around the tent.

Just outside the opening of the tent was a cooler table full of ice and an assortment of drinks. Under that table were a couple of metal barrels full of wine and champagne as well.

Each table was covered with a white tablecloth and as a centerpiece each had a vase full of beautiful purple and white flowers, next to a clear vase full of candles. There were champagne glasses turned upside down around the vases in anticipation of the Champagne Toast. And at each place setting there was a little white box wrapped in purple ribbons that held a memento of the day. It was a clear shot glass with a purple butterfly on each side. On top of the butterfly it simply read Karen and Eddie and below was the date of this occasion.

The chairs for observing the Event were set up in perfect rows. Most of them were on the parquet like flooring of the dance floor, just leaving enough of an aisle for us to walk down

Sonja, the Minister, was setting up a camera on a tripod right where we would recite our vows to each other. And next to her the DJ was setting up his equipment for the evening. Eddie was chatting with the guests then as I snuck away upstairs with my daughters and my sisters to prepare.

I checked my hair and my makeup and then slipped into my dress with my daughter's help. My dress was purple of course, very simple but elegant. It had three quarter length sleeves which turned out to be perfect for the cool weather that day. It had a rather low neckline to allow just the appropriate amount of cleavage. The hemline came to just above my knees and I wore Barbie like black sandals with a wedged heel so that I wouldn't sink into the grass in the yard.

I wanted my jewelry to accent the simplicity of my dress. I'd found a perfect bracelet. It was rather wide with clear and purple stones that gave just the right amount of bling. My earrings were also made up of clear gemstones that dropped down below my hair and my necklace was a shiny silver herringbone chain.

My sister Nancy stopped taking photos long enough to say, "Karen, give me your bouquet for just a moment."

As I handed it to her, I remembered.

Since my mother had passed away many years before, Nancy had started a tradition. She held onto a beautiful opal ring that belonged to my mom. She brought it to all our daughters' weddings and now mine to be a part of the day. It was that "something old" that was traditional. Underneath the flowers of the bouquet near the ribbon wrapped base that I'd hold, she pinned the ring. The bouquet was beautiful. It was full of white roses and freesia in several shades of purple.

Nancy looked at me and said, "Okay, mom is with us here now to help us celebrate this day."

We hugged as our eyes welled up with tears. You could see them in the photos that my daughter took at that moment.

She said, "Okay, enough of that. Your guests are waiting downstairs."

There was a knock on my bedroom door then. It was my son who was getting impatient to walk me down the aisle. "Are you ready to go? It's almost time," he said.

When he saw me there in front of the mirror, his face lit up. He walked right up to me and hugged me and said, "You look pretty mommy."

My sisters snapped a few more photos then of me and my three kids. We'd been through so much together, the four of us to get to this point in all our lives. Finally we were living the way that we should be, happy and peaceful and calm. We didn't have to pretend anymore that we were part of a happy family because now we were... finally. The smiles on our faces were so genuine, from the inside out. We radiated. And now Ed would make our family whole.

My daughters looked so beautiful. They wore similar dresses. They were knee length and both of them were black and beige. They looked very elegant. And my son looked so handsome and so happy. He wore a chocolate colored jacket with black pants and a black shirt. We all radiated.

From the window, we heard the DJ say, "Would everyone please take a seat under the tent now? The ceremony is about to begin."

My sisters ran down the stairs then and shooed a few more stragglers who were still in the house to the tent outside. The four of us lined up then for our entrance as I could hear the chosen song begin to play. It was an instrumental version of the Beatles "PS I Love You." It seemed so appropriate.

My heart was pounding so hard; I was so excited. The moment had finally arrived.

My two daughters, one at a time, walked through the open patio doors outside onto the deck, down the stairs and between the rows of guests to the waiting Minister and to Eddie.

Just at that moment, as my son and I stood around the corner of the open patio door, I had "The Moment" I'd predicted in my mind every time I'd thought of this day finally happening. My dream come true was happening right now. My eyes filled with tears and I couldn't move. I was frozen for a couple of moments.

I said to my son, "I can't believe this is happening. I knew this would be the moment that this would all hit me."

He said, "Tears of joy mom?"

"Of course, tears of my dream coming true." I said.

"You need a hug mommy?"

"I do," I said with a smile.

He gave me a huge hug then. It was all I needed.

"Let's do this, I'm ready."

As we walked out the door and down the stairs, I laughed as I said to him, "Please just don't let me fall, hold onto me."

He laughed too as he said, "No worries mom, I've got you."

I know that everyone was looking my way as I walked down the aisle but all I could see was Eddie. As I got closer to him, I noticed once again the way the one side of his lips curls up just a bit more than the other side when he first begins to smile. And those beautiful blue eyes of his were just sparkling in the sunshine. I could tell by the way that he looked at me just how much he liked what he saw. I couldn't stop smiling at him and he couldn't stop smiling at me.

As Sonja took my arm to direct me to the exact spot where she wanted me to stand, I noticed for just a moment out of the corner of my eye, the movement of people with cameras around me. I don't know who they were but nothing else mattered at this moment but me and Eddie. The music stopped.

Eddie and I faced each other than and I held his hands as he held mine. We looked into each other's eyes and listened to what the preacher said.

She began, "We are gathered together on this beautiful afternoon to witness the Marriage of Karen and Eddie. Through their Friendship together, a love has grown, filling both of their lives with a greater enthusiasm and joy for life. Surely it must have been fate that brought them together, Eddie in New York and Karen in Chicago. What started out as a Split Second Chance Meeting grew into an overwhelming Love and devotion for each other."

I held Eddie's hands even tighter as we began our vows.

Eddie said, "In the Spirit of Love and Unity, I Eddie, marry you Karen, merging my life and its purpose with yours and shall endeavor to love and honor you as long as we both shall live. Like I said when I first knew that I loved you, all you have to do each day is to get up and breathe; I'll do all the rest. You are my Queen and I vow to treat you as such. I Love You."

I responded, "In the Spirit of Love and Unity, I Karen, marry you Eddie, merging my life and its purpose with yours and shall endeavor to love and honor you as long as we both shall live. I am so proud to be standing here next to you. I never knew that love like ours existed. You are my Knight in Shining Armor. You rode by on your White Horse and you swept me off my feet. I Love You."

We exchanged rings and before we knew it, Sonja said, "Under the Ordinance of God and by the Authority vested in me by the state of Illinois, I now pronounce you Husband and Wife. You may kiss the bride."

As we kissed, all the guests began to clap and cheer us on. The music began; a very upbeat happy version of, "I'm a Believer."

As the five of us turned around to face the Guests, it was so joyful. Eddie gave the thumbs up sign to all, to which everyone laughed and cheered even louder.

We walked right over to the side of the yard with the huge Evergreens to start taking photos while my helpers moved all the chairs and poured the Champagne and set up all the food.

After about half an hour of picture taking, it was time to have dinner. My children and their partners and Eddie and I sat at the head table in the tent. There was lots of talking and music and laughing going on when the DJ announced, "Everyone please have a seat, it's time for the Champagne Toasts."

My brother did the first. He started, "When Karen first asked me to do this I thought it was a roast, it turned out to be a toast so here goes."

My brother is a comedian; he thinks he is anyway. His toast turned out to be so sweet.

He said, "I did some research to find some inspirational words so I looked up a couple of authors. One is long forgotten and one is brand new and not well known. We will start with that one. This author has said, 'I'm a firm believer in no guts, no glory. Listen to your inner voices; they really know what they are talking about. Take a chance; dreams really do come true.' All of these phrases seem to apply to Karen and Eddie's happiness now. What a wise *author*."

I laughed as I realized that the *author* he was talking about was me. All these quotes were mine. I felt complimented.

He went on to say, "Here's what the long forgotten author said. 'Eddie and Karen sittin in a tree,' " to which every one of my guests roared with laughter, he continued, "K- I –S- S- I- N -G!" And then even louder till everyone joined him, "Karen and Eddie sittin in a tree K- I- S- S -I -N - G!"

He finished then saying, "May Karen and Eddie have many, many years of sitting up in the tree and loving each other and loving life."

The DJ next introduced Eddie's sister who also gave the sweetest toast.

She said, "In all the years of knowing my brother, I have never once seen him as happy as he is today." And as we could hear her get choked up she said, "Karen I have to thank you for that." She went on to say, "I have more contact with him now than I ever did before and I live in New York and he's here a thousand miles away and I also want to thank Karen for that. I hope that you both have a long, wonderful and happy life together. You both deserve it."

After dinner that night Eddie and I danced the first dance to one of our favorite romantic songs. We thought for sure when we chose it that it would make us cry but it was so meaningful to us, that we had to play it. It turned out we didn't cry at all. As I danced with him, with all our guests around us, I saw no one but him, my Eddie, My Knight in Shining Armor.

The song went, "Lying here with you, listening to the rain, smiling just to see the smile upon your face. These are the moments I thank God that I'm alive. These are the moments, I'll remember all my life. I found all I've waited for and I could not ask for more."

That was the best day of my life so far. I will never forget it. I take such comfort in knowing that I've documented this whole love story with Eddie. Now I know that when I'm old and gray, even if I lose my memory in my head, I have this story that I can read to remind me. I don't ever want to forget a single thing.

***

Three weeks later we celebrated again in New York with Eddie's friends who I'm happy to call mine now. We had a mini reception. We had another cake made for us that said, "Mr. and Mrs." The whole group gave us a Scrabble game amongst other gifts to celebrate the occasion. I didn't even realize that I was crying as we opened it until I felt the tears running down my nose.

Happiness like this I've never known.

Eddie and I are firm believers now that life is so short that we want to celebrate our love every day. There's something about our whole story that makes people feel good; makes them sigh and smile.

I'd marry Eddie every day if I could and I know that it won't be more than a couple of years down the road before we will celebrate our Anniversary in a big way with all our family and friends again.

I still can't believe this whole thing happened to me. I feel like I'm living someone else's life sometimes. I'm thrilled when I realize that it's mine.

I can't believe some of the things I've done to get to where I am today but I am so grateful that I did.

Just as I felt compelled by some power greater than myself to take a chance and meet Eddie, I also felt compelled to write this, as I was so inspired by this love story that's become my life. I felt it was my obligation to share this story of hope and inspiration and love with all of you.

151

A B O U T T H E A U T H O R

K AREN L BONCELA LIVES in a suburb just outside of Chicago with her husband. She is a mother of three grown children, a grandma to one so far and a New Author, having been inspired for the first time to write after having met her "Knight in Shining Armor."

You can visit Karen at *facebook.com/wordstoloveby.klb.*
Email her at *kared8111@hotmail.com.*
See Karen's Tweets at *Karenlboncela@twitter.com.*

Karen and Eddie

www.ingramcontent.com/pod-product-compliance
Lightning Source LLC
LaVergne TN
LVHW011237080426
835509LV00005B/539